ABOUT THE AUTHOR

Larry Richards has the education needed to write on the Book of Hebrews. He graduated with honors from Dallas Theological Seminary. Before that he earned a degree in philosophy from the University of Michigan, graduating magna cum laude. Later, he earned a Ph.D. from Northwestern University.

Richards also has the experience needed to make the Book of Hebrews relevant to daily living. A former professor of Christian Education at Wheaton College, he now lives in Phoenix, Arizona, from where he writes and speaks in the interest of revitalizing the local church.

His ability to communicate biblical truth clearly has resulted in a number of books with the Richards byline. Victor Books has published several of these, including *Becoming One in the Spirit*, *U-Turn* (a study of Luke's Gospel), and *Born to Grow* (a book "for new and used Christians").

The Complete Christian

Insights for life from the Book of Hebrews

Larry Richards

This book is designed for your personal reading pleasure and profit. It is also designed for group study. A leader's guide with helps and hints for teachers and visual aids (Victor Multiuse Transparency Masters) is available from your local bookstore or from the publisher.

VICTOR BOOKS

a division of SP Publications, Inc.
WHEATON, ILLINOIS 60187

Offices also in Fullerton, California • Whitby, Ontario, Canada • Amersham-on-the-Hill, Bucks, England

Eighth printing, 1981

Library of Congress Catalog Card No. 74-84617

ISBN 0-88207-714-7

VICTOR BOOKS
A division of SP Publications, Inc.
P.O. Box 1825 • Wheaton, Ill. 60187

CONTENTS

FOUNDATION TRUTHS
  1. The Whole Truth (Heb. 1)   7
  2. Focus on Me! (Heb. 2)   18
  3. We Try Harder? (Heb. 3:1—4:13)   29
  4. Linked! (Heb. 4:14—5:14)   44
  5. The Full Experience (Heb. 6)   56

DEEPER TRUTHS (IDENTITY)
  6. Guaranteed! (Heb. 7)   67
  7. Written Within (Heb. 8:1—9:10)   77
  8. Holy! (Heb. 9:11—10:25)   90
  9. "Hurry up" Faith (Heb. 10:26-39)   101

DEEPER TRUTHS (LIFE)
  10. By Faith (Heb. 11)   114
  11. With Discipline (Heb. 12)   125
  12. In Love (Heb. 13)   136

1

THE WHOLE TRUTH

The pastor of a Seattle church was talking about some new believers in his congregation. "They've only been with us about a year, so of course they haven't got it all together yet."

I couldn't help smiling. How many Christians ever do feel that they've "got it all together"? How many of us are really sure . . . sure that we understand what God is doing in our lives, sure that we're growing toward maturity, sure that we're experiencing all that God has made possible for us? Isn't it more common that we have fragments of truth, and experience fragments of the blessings Jesus came to bring?

This idea of fragments begins the Book of Hebrews. In the very first sentence, the writer reminds his Jewish-Christian readers that God spoke to their forefathers at many times and in various ways. The word translated "many times," *polumeros*, means literally "many parts." Fragments. In bits and pieces. God revealed throughout the Old Testament many glimpses of truth

. . . but the revelation was always incomplete. God's people rejoiced in the fragments, and trusted Him. But they were not privileged to grasp the whole.

And then Jesus came. "In these last days" (Heb. 1:2) God spoke to us by His Son. In Jesus, you and I were given the whole truth. We were invited to put our lives all together in Him. We were given, in Jesus, both the whole truth, and a personal invitation to wholeness!

Fragmented Lives

This awareness is what seems to have bothered the writer of the letter to the Hebrews. Jesus, the whole Truth, had invited men to an exciting wholeness and joy, a true fulfillment that comes with maturity. But somehow many people who had come to trust Jesus as Saviour were missing out on the full benefit of their salvation. They had taken that first vital step of trust in Christ, which assured their eternal salvation, but they were missing out on the exciting daily growth that is a part of present salvation.

They were saved. But they were missing half of what salvation means! And they found that being "halfway" saved isn't exciting at all.

What do we know about the people to whom the Book of Hebrews was written? We know that they were second generation Christians (2:3) who had been an established church for some time (see 10:32; 13:7). While they had not yet suffered intense persecution (12:4), things hadn't been easy for them (10:32-34). For some, the new faith had meant prison and economic loss.

We know that they had been Christians long

enough to become mature (5:12), but had somehow missed the way.

We know too, from the whole tone of the letter,
that the men and women of this Hebrew-
Christian congregation were wondering about
what they had given up—and what they had
gained. They were looking back longingly at the
old ways of Judaism, at the traditional pattern of
life that had seemed so stable and secure. They
were wondering if the way of life they had left
wasn't perhaps better than the new one they had
adopted.

We can sympathize with their uncertainty and
their unhappiness. The Old Testament faith bore
the stamp of divine revelation. God had spoken
through prophets, through angels, through history itself, and through acts that were clearly
miraculous. He had spoken by means of the seven
annual festivals of worship that marked the
Hebrew year, and in the sacrifices that dealt with
sin and gave the worshiper a way to express praise
and thanksgiving. He had spoken in the closely
regulated way of life of the committed Jew, and in
the divine Law, which expressed the highest
moral tone. A man who was born a Jew and whose
heart was warm toward God found in the total
pattern of life under the Old Testament a great
sense of fulfillment and identity.

But then Jesus came—the Messiah the prophets
had foretold—promising a salvation that included
but went beyond the glimpses given in the Old
Testament. These Hebrew men and women had
believed in Him. Turning from what they had
known all their lives, they had ventured out to
discover a new way of life and a new identity.
And then, somehow, the venture threatened to

turn sour. They had tried, but they had missed the
way to maturity. They had missed the *wholeness*.
They had found more *fragments* of truth, but they
had been unable to put it all together and to
discover in Jesus a new life and identity more
fulfilling than the old.

Find Wholeness

Perhaps your experience has been like this too.
It's not at all unusual. We come to Jesus, and at
first there's a glow of excitement. The things we
hear taught from the Bible are new and wonderful
to us. Our lives and attitudes change. We can see
growth.

But somehow *everything* doesn't change—not
the way we thought it would. Somehow we're still
the same inside. Somehow we can't seem to get
the fragments together into that whole new way
of life that is truly *Christian*. Then there comes a
time when we know we aren't growing any
longer, when the excitement seems to drain away.
We begin to wonder. Is *this* all there is to being a
Christian? Isn't there more?

The Book of Hebrews insists that there *is* more.
It was written to people who have somehow
missed the way to maturity and are stumbling. It
was written to help us put our fragments of faith in
Jesus all together into a fully satisfying whole,
and to move us out to *experience* the fullness of
this complete salvation. Jesus put together all the
fragments of truth about God to give us the whole
truth. But more than that, Jesus also puts fragmented lives together, to give us wholeness and
maturity as persons. In Hebrews, we can discover
all these treasures!

Full Disclosure
Hebrews 1:1-3

Salvation begins with Jesus. This is how the Book of Hebrews begins too. Total confidence in Jesus is the basis for our new life and identity as "Christians."

It was particularly important to begin with Jesus in writing to these Hebrew Christians. The Hebrew Scriptures had given glimpses of the truth that the "God of Abraham, Isaac, and Jacob," as the Jews most often identified Him, was really one God in three Persons.

However, the doctrine of the Trinity was never explicitly taught in the Old Testament. It could be glimpsed in the plurals of Genesis 1, as God said, "Let *us* make man in *our* image" (v. 26). It could be detected in the very term by which the unity of God was affirmed each Sabbath in the synagogue: "Hear, O Israel! The Lord is our God, the Lord is one" (Deut. 6:4, NASB). That *one* in the original permits a compound unity, such as that of a single bunch of grapes which is composed of numerous units. Glimpses of the Trinity could also be seen in the many Old Testament references to the Spirit of God as distinct from God Himself.

Yet, only when Jesus came and taught "I and the Father are one" (John 10:30) was truth about God as three Persons fully disclosed. When it was disclosed, and Jesus began to explain that "no one comes to the Father except through Me" (John 14:6), it became vitally important that believers learn to rest their full confidence in Him.

It also became important to realize that *all there is* of salvation for us is to be found in Jesus. There is nothing higher or greater than knowing Jesus.

There is nothing beyond knowing Jesus that is key to a supposedly "higher" spiritual experience. The Bible says of the Holy Spirit, "He will bring glory to Me [Jesus]" (John 16:14). In everything in our Christian lives, God has determined that the focus should be on Jesus. We can come to know Jesus better . . . but we can never find anything better than knowing Jesus.

So it's important for us to begin with an accurate impression of Jesus. This impression will be enriched and expanded throughout the Book of Hebrews. Yet the initial picture of Him must be sharp and clear. Our initial picture must leave no doubts that Jesus is God.

Sonship belongs to Jesus (v. 2). This term has been used by some to question the full deity of Jesus. But the term *son* is designed to emphasize relationships between the Persons of the Godhead, not to suggest that Jesus is a created being. Even the term *firstborn* (1:6), according to Arndt and Gingrich's Greek Lexicon, "is admirably suited to describe Jesus as the One coming forth from God to found the new community of saints" (p. 734). He is "firstborn" in that He is the founder, the model, the one with the Father's full authority to act (see Rev. 1:5; Rom. 8:29).

The clearest evidence for Jesus' position as a full member of the Godhead is given in these early verses, as we see who Jesus is, all He accomplished, and all that will be His.

The coming kingdom belongs to Jesus (v. 2). Jesus has been "appointed Heir to all things." He will inherit and purify this world at His coming, and then create a new heaven and new earth. He is Heir to all, and this constitutes a promise that one day all will be fully God's.

Creative power belongs to Jesus (v. 2). Jesus is the One who spoke, and in speaking caused our whole vast universe to appear. Jesus is the One who billions of years ago acted to shape stars so distant that astronomers can only guess at their existence.

The original glory of God belongs to Jesus (v. 3). The phrases "radiance of God's glory" and "the exact representation of His Being" are both strong assertions. Radiance, the light shining forth from a luminary, is all that the human eye can see. Similarly, all that we can see of God shines through Jesus! *Exact representation* assures us that there is a total and complete correspondence between the eternal God and the Man Jesus. If you and I look at Jesus, we see exactly what God is like, for He is the full and exact revelation of God.

Sustaining power belongs to Jesus (v. 3). Even today the entire universe would flicker and flame out of existence were it not for the power of Jesus, energizing the so-called "natural laws" that govern our physical universe.

Redemptive work belongs to Jesus (v. 3). Jesus not only is the active agent in all that is accomplished in the physical universe; He also acts in the moral and personal realm. It was He who provided purification from sins, and thus opened up to us the possibility of a new and whole life.

Exaltation belongs to Jesus (v. 3). As a Man, Jesus walked our earth and knew our nature and weaknesses. But now, once again, He was returned to "the right hand of the Majesty in heaven." His work has been fully accomplished. He rests now, knowing that He *has provided* a salvation able to make us whole. Now, seeing

Him restored to majesty, the focus of our praise and worship, we need to learn to rest in the fact that He is God.

Greater Than Angels
Hebrews 1:4-14

It may seem strange. After this quick sketch of Jesus' deity the Book of Hebrews goes on to point out His superiority to angels. But perhaps it's not so strange after all.

From time to time, there is a great renewal of interest in the occult. Even Christians are sometimes intrigued by the possibility of getting "inside information" on future events from supposedly angelic sources. Even Christians sometimes turn to the occult when they sense a need for special guidance. For people who believe in the supernatural, it's not too great a step when uncertain about God's will to turn to some other supernatural source, wondering if perhaps God will speak to them through it.

Of course, those who know the Bible realize that God has decisively cut us off from the occult as an avenue to discovery of His will (see Deut. 18:10-22). In Old Testament times, God sent prophets to reveal His will—a revelation we have recorded for our benefit in the Old Testament's 39 books. He also promised *The Prophet* would come . . . One who would *fully* reveal Him. Since Jesus has come and given that complete disclosure, and the canon of Scripture has been closed, we need no "extra" supernatural source of information.

However, the Jewish attitude toward angels involved even more than we have yet suggested.

Barclay points out that "in New Testament times the Jews believed that God gave the law first to angels and that the angels passed it on to Moses because direct communication between man and God was unthinkable (see Acts 7:53; Gal. 3:19)" (*The Letter to the Hebrews*, Wm. Barclay, The Westminster Press, Philadelphia, Pa.). The angels were created beings who were higher than men, and closer to God, and *they* were thus thought to be the intermediaries between God and men.

The Bible tells us that angels are beings with individual personalities and names. They were created by God before man was created. These spiritual beings do not have physical bodies like ours, though they can appear to us and act in the material world. Angels were created in order to minister (Heb. 1:14) and to carry out God's will. For instance, we see an angel releasing Peter from jail in Acts 5. However, not all angels are "good" angels. The Bible tells us that Lucifer, an angel, chose to sin and became Satan. A number of angels followed him in rebellion (see 2 Peter 2:4). These fallen angels are the "demons" we read of in the Bible and in occult literature.

The Hebrew Christians, aware of the Bible's teaching about angels and aware that angels had been God's messengers in the past, found it difficult to accept fully the fact that in Jesus God had established direct communication, had come to speak to us personally, face to face. There was a temptation in the Early Church to think of Jesus as a "high" angel . . . surely someone great, but God Himself? To counter this, the writer of Hebrews makes sure at the outset that we realize that Jesus is totally superior to all the angels, for He is God!

Superior relationship (v. 5). Jesus stands *beside* God the Father as His Son—not *below* Him as a creature.

Superior as Deity (vv. 6-9). None of the angels is called God, and no angel is worshiped by his fellows. Yet Jesus is given the name of God, and the angelic hosts worship Him.

Superior as Creator (vv. 10-12). Like the angels (who are immortal, not knowing birth and death as we do) Jesus will outlast the universe. Unlike angels, however, He was there "in the beginning," when He laid the foundations of creation. Angels change and grow in knowledge as the centuries unfold God's plan, but Jesus remains the same; as God He knows all.

Superior in destiny (v. 13). No angel was ever invited to share the rule of the universe as God's equal. But for God to picture Jesus, "at My right hand," indicates that Jesus shares God's rule even now.

In every way Jesus is superior—and thus it must be that the revelation He brings, and the salvation He offers, is superior to the fragments offered in the Old Testament. There is no need to look elsewhere. In Jesus we have the whole truth . . . and in Jesus the best possibility of being made whole ourselves.

A New Identity
Hebrews 1:14

But what is it that Jesus offers us? What will it involve? We see a hint in verse 14: "Are not all angels ministering spirits sent to serve those who will inherit salvation?"

The Jews had looked up to angels as superior

beings. Now, in one verse, Hebrews opens up a whole new line of thought. Angels are merely *servants* of those who will inherit salvation. Whatever we may be in ourselves, salvation lifts us above the angels! The Scripture puts it this way: Jesus was made "a little lower than the angels" (2:9) *for a time* . . . that He might bring *us* to glory. Salvation lifts us out of ourselves and carries us to a new life in Him.

What is this new life like? What does it mean for us to be lifted beyond ourselves to claim a share of glory? We can't tell yet. But as we go on in Hebrews, and discover the full salvation God has planned for us, we're likely to find God's wholeness is far more than we've ever dreamed or desired.

Can we be *sure* of it? Yes, for God is done now with fragments. He has spoken at last in His Son, and in Jesus we have the whole.

EXPLORE

To further explore this portion of Scripture and its meaning for you . . .

1. Look again at the things Hebrews 1:1-4 says about Jesus. Which helps you feel most confidence in Him—and why?

2. What images of a life of wholeness does the phrase "above the angels" create for you? What kind of life do you think Jesus intends to give you?

3. What are some of the characteristics of Jesus seen in 1:5-13 that you might expect to see reproduced in believers? What are some you would not expect to see reproduced even in "heirs of salvation?"

2

FOCUS ON ME!

Our Tuesday night group was studying Hebrews two, and we began by talking about this question: "What, to you, has been the most important thing about being saved?"

What reply would you have given to that question?

We got a variety of answers. Hope. Peace. Assurance of hell avoided and heaven promised. Knowing I'm in God's good graces and not hovering between heaven and hell. Knowing I don't have to wait to be saved; that it's a daily thing now. Knowing Jesus and growing personally. A sense of meaning to life, and a solid foundation. They were all good answers, and it was exciting to see that knowing Jesus did have real meaning to each of us.

As, no doubt, it has to you.

But as we went on in the chapter, we saw that each of the answers was incomplete. Each fell short of expressing the fantastic impact of the salvation that God has chosen to focus on us.

Neglect
Hebrews 2:1-4

This chapter begins with a warning. It's a warning about neglecting and losing sight of what the writer is going to tell us about salvation. The first verse is important, and the key expressions *pay careful attention* and *drift away* are both nautical terms. We could accurately translate it, "We must eagerly anchor ourselves to the truths we've been taught, or we're likely to drift away from our moorings."

Actually, this is just what the Hebrew Christians were doing. They had carelessly allowed themselves to slip away from the full meaning of their salvation in Christ. As a result, they were considering a return to Judaism.

We find it easy to fall into similar error. Life gets hurried and busy. We plunge into a round of activities—sometimes they are church activities. And we carelessly slip away from the real meaning of our salvation. Then, suddenly, we become aware that our life has lost its savor. The joy is gone. We cast about anxiously, wondering what is wrong.

In the Book of Hebrews we can rediscover, with the first readers, what the foundation truths of the Gospel are. And we are invited with them to sink the anchor of our lives deep into the reality that this inspired Book goes on to describe.

In looking at these first verses of chapter two, then, we see that they do not relate to the question of "being lost" after a person is saved, but with the danger to the believer of drifting away from the full meaning of his salvation. This ignoring of the gift of God would cause his life on earth to lose its taste and meaning.

To strengthen the warning, the writer points out that the Old Testament message, which was mediated by angels, involved a just punishment when those who heard it either wilfully or carelessly violated its principles. Now Jesus has come with a far greater message: greater in that it came personally from Him without mediation; greater in God's authentication of the message by miraculous signs; greater in the inner transformation that salvation produces in believers. Certainly letting ourselves drift from the truths of this Gospel will have disastrous results.

What Is Man?
Hebrews 2:5-9

With the warning given, and the exhortation to anchor our lives solidly in the great realities of the salvation Jesus brings, the writer moves on to consider another important entity.

And what does he talk about?

Man.

In chapter one the writer began with Jesus. Salvation means we must grasp clearly who Jesus, the Son of God, is.

In this chapter the writer focuses on us. To understand salvation and to avoid slipping into a life of frustration and spiritual immaturity, we must grasp who *we* are.

The writer begins with a quote from Psalm 8 (see vv. 4-6). As Barclay notes, "If we are ever to understand this passage correctly, we must understand one thing—*the whole reference of Psalm 8 is to man.*" In describing the glory and honor God has given to man, the writer makes it clear that God destined you and me to be like kings!

Probably our first reaction to this idea is to draw back. We're so used to understanding ourselves primarily as sinners. We're so deeply aware of our inadequacies. What psychologists call a "poor self-image" often dominates us and as a result we hesitate to risk action for fear that failure will certainly follow. Sometimes we even excuse our failure to respond to God's Word with the agonizing excuse, "I can't!" A sense of our weakness and inability distorts our lives and destroys our trust.

It is just this sense of failure and inadequacy that the writer of Hebrews begins to attack now. The truth about man is critical to our understanding of the message of salvation, and we must never grow careless and let awareness of who we really are slip away.

Man's destiny. The writer begins with a jolting thought. God hasn't subjected the coming world to angels. He has reserved that glory for you and me. In the original creation (Gen. 1:26-27), God stated His intention to make man "in Our image, according to Our Likeness" and to give man dominion.

Scripture states it very strongly: "In putting everything under him, God left nothing that is not subject to him" (Heb. 2:8). Man is king.

The psalmist understood the high destiny of humanity, and cried out in wonder: "What is man that You are concerned about him?" Yet God was and is concerned about us. Concerned enough to crown us with "glory and honor."

Man's state. The emphasis in this passage is on what man was created to be and is destined to be. But it is clear that, right now, we aren't what we were meant to be. "At present we do not see everything subject to him" (v. 8). Our destiny has been interrupted, our identity clouded by sin. With sin, the whole world has flown out of control, and we ourselves have lost our glory and have become slaves. *Yet, it is the present weak and helpless state of human beings that is distorted and unreal.* It is the poor self-image that is out of harmony with the reality of eternity, for we *will* see man restored and we will see the world to come subjected to him.

God's remedy. We can dimly see our lost glory. We can all too clearly see the frustration and defeat we know today. What else can we see? "We see Jesus" (v. 9). We see Jesus who became a man, becoming for a time a little lower than the angels. We see Him suffering death for us. And we see Him raised, "crowned with glory and honor."

We see in Jesus a Man who has been restored to the dominion and glory God intended for us all. And, in Jesus, we are to see ourselves!

Barclay sums up the three basic ideas of this passage. "(1) God created man, only a little less than Himself, to have the mastery over all things. (2) Man through his sin entered into frustration and defeat instead of mastery and dominion. (3) Into this state of frustration and defeat came Jesus Christ, in order that by His life and death and glory, He might make man what man was meant to be."

What the Book of Hebrews is telling us, then, is this: "Now that you are saved, you must never let slip the awareness that you are no longer a defeated and frustrated being. Because of Jesus you have been—and are being— restored to the experience of dominion and mastery for which God always intended man."

To see yourself accurately, you need to see not the slave made impotent by sin, but the renewed man who has a restored capacity for dominion and who, in Christ, is master of life.

You need to see yourself as *undefeated*.

Dominion Start here Dec 20
Hebrews 2:10-18

These few verses emphasize truths that are stunning in their vast impact. They tell of an amazing transaction, an amazing transmutation. They tell us first that Jesus, determined to rescue us, took a full share of our humanity and through His death released us from our slavery. They tell us that, in that identification with us, Jesus also identified us with Him. He, the Son of God, became a man, that you and I might become sons of God! He entered the family of man that we might enter the family of God!

Because of what Jesus accomplished, we now must learn to see ourselves for who we are: the very brothers of Jesus Christ and through our relationship with Him the children of God the Father.

We are not merely men restored to the original glory. We are men and women who have been raised to share the holiness and the glory of God as members of the divine family (2:10-11).

We are slaves no longer. We are defeated no longer. We have been granted His power to be free, the ability to live victoriously.

The following chart summarizes the transformation that this passage describes and also picks up the discussion of the first chapter about our relationship with angels. Looking at it, we can see that our present position is with Jesus "in the heavenlies" (see Eph. 1:3; 2:6; 3:10), a truth we are to learn to live by.

Hebrews 1 and 2 describe our relationship with angels and Jesus. He "was made a little lower than the angels" for a time (2:9), that He might bring *us* to glory. We can chart it like this:

original	incarnation	resurrection
Jesus		Jesus/us
↓		↓
angels — — — — — —	angels — — — — — —	angels
↓	↓	
us	Jesus/us	

Jesus is not only exalted above the angels, He has lifted us up to share this destiny with Him! To experience the full meaning of salvation we must never drift from the amazing truth that, in Christ, we *now* have the capacity for mastery and dominion.

FIGURE 1

In the family (vv. 10-13). The new position that Jesus brings us as sons of God is so unexpected that the writer repeats it over and over.

Jesus brought "many sons to glory."

Believers and Jesus are "of the same family."

Jesus "is not ashamed to call them brothers."

Jesus "will declare Your [God's] name to My brothers."

We are "the children God has given Me [Jesus]."

These family terms make it clear that our identity is no longer rooted in our old relationship to Adam (through whom the bondage and frustration we've known came), but that our new identity is rooted in our relationship to Jesus. We are to discover ourselves as sons of God and brothers of Christ. We are to learn to live out that relationship just as earlier we lived out our relationship to Adam as sinners.

What, then, does living out our new relationship to God involve? What does "being saved" mean to us if we accept ourselves as new persons in Christ? Verse 11 records it: "The One who *makes men holy* and those *who are made holy* are of the same family." Being saved means that we are to share God's holiness. *We are to be like Him.*

Peter puts it plainly. "Live as obedient children before God. Don't let your character be molded by the desires of your ignorant days, but be holy in every department of your lives, for the One who has called you is Himself holy" (1 Peter 1:14-15, PH). He goes on to explain: "For you are sons of God now; the live, permanent Word of the living God has given you His own indestructible heredity" (1:23, PH).

You are no longer merely mortals.

You have been given God's heredity.

You are a brother of Jesus; you are a child of God. And as a member of God's family, you are called to be like Him.

It is this, perhaps, that most clearly helps us see the maturity and fulfillment that the Bible, and Hebrews in particular, describes for us. God has called us to grow more and more like Him in every area of our lives. And for this kind of growth, we must never forget who Jesus is—and we must never let slip our awareness of who we are in Him.

We are no longer the frustrated, impotent persons we were before we trusted Jesus. We have been lifted above all that. We have been raised to mastery.

Full humanity (vv. 14-16). The Bible goes on to

make it clear that we were enabled to share fully in all that God is only because Jesus, in becoming a human being, shared fully in all that we are. He actually became a man, so that His death as a man might destroy Satan's power over man, a power that operated through death and the fear of death. It was the fear of death, the Bible says, that previously held us in slavery. Not just the end of our life on earth seems to be in view here. Someone has said, "Every time I fail, I die a little." It is the constant realization of helplessness, summed up in the final death of the body no matter how we may struggle against it, that creates fear in us, and makes us cringe away from the future and from change.

But with Jesus' death, that fear and Satan who wielded its power have been done away. We need no longer fear death, because we now have been given life—eternal life. And this not only promises endless existence, but also promises the power to live now.

The writer can't resist another reminder. "Surely it is not angels He helps, but Abraham's descendants" (v. 16). It is not the angels that God is concerned with. It is you and me ... individuals who, like Abraham, place our faith in Him, and through faith are given His life (see Rom. 4:12).

The experience gap (vv. 17-18). The final verses of the chapter introduce two new thoughts. The first is the recognition that there is a gap between our present *experience* and our present *position*. We are Christ's brothers, raised with Him into the heavenlies. But as we live our life on earth, we sometimes act out of the old relationship with Adam. We may continue to sin and slip into the frustration of the defeated way of life we knew before we met Jesus. For this, we need continual atonement (v. 17). We need continual forgiveness.

And we need help.

This is the second thought. Because Jesus actually did become a human being, "made like His brothers in every way," He is able to sympathize with us. He can identify with us in our need.

It takes a man who has known hunger to sympathize with the hungry. It takes a man who has known the joy and pain of love to enter into the experience of lovers. It takes a man who has known rejection to feel the pain of the defeated. Jesus became a human being in the fullest sense, and "because He Himself suffered when He was tempted, He is able to help those who are being tempted." The need that we feel for help, to break out of the trap we find ourselves in and to live as the new men God says we are, is something Jesus does not condemn. He understands. And He is "able to help."

This is what is so exciting about the Book of Hebrews. In it God shows us our destiny and reveals the new identity we bear as His children. And then God goes on to show us *how Jesus helps us* to actually *experience* the victory He has won. Hebrews chapter two says, "Realize who you are!" And then the book goes on to show how Jesus, the source of our new identity, constantly reaches out to bring our experience into harmony with who we are.

EXPLORE

To further explore this portion of Scripture and its meaning to you . . .

1. Read Psalm 8 and jot down your impression of how God views man.

2. How do you feel about yourself? Using crayons to express yourself, creatively draw the "real you."

3. Reread this chapter, and evaluate your portrait (above). As a Christian, who are you *really*? How might you draw yourself as God sees you in Christ?

4. Reread chapter 2 of Hebrews. Discover benefits of salvation that are future—and benefits that are to be enjoyed now. What do these benefits mean to you today?

3

WE TRY HARDER!

Bret is a big, bluff but gentle guy who was saved in his 40s. Looking back over his earlier life, his sins and mistakes, the way he hurt others and hurt God, Bret has come to feel that he has much to make up for.

As a result, Bret has thrown himself into his Christian life. He takes on more and more offices at church. He gets up early for Christian businessmen's meetings. He attends conferences and study groups. He's turned off the TV and turned on to Christian books and periodicals. But somehow the frantic round of activities does not bring him peace. There are still strains in the family. There is still a nagging sense of guilt over the wasted years. When you talk with Bret about the Christian life as a "rest," he struggles to understand . . . he yearns to experience it . . . but he seems unable to do anything but "try harder."

The rest for the people of God, described in Hebrews 3 and 4, eludes him.

It eluded the men and women who first re-

Matthew 11 - 28
Come unto me all you who are weary and burdened
and I will give you rest.

ceived these Scriptures too. They had not only lost sight of their identity in Christ, but they had also wandered from the simple, yet exciting principles of the way of life Jesus called them to share. If you've ever known the agonies of the "try harder" Christian life, these chapters are definitely for you.

Greater Than Moses
Hebrews 3:1-6

The writer introduces this section about the way those who "have come to share in Christ" (3:14) are to live their new lives by pointing out that Christ is far superior to Moses.

There are two reasons for introducing Moses at this point. The first is that the Jews revered Moses as greater even than the angels. Rabbi Jose ben Chalafta, commenting on Numbers 12:6-7, from which Hebrews quotes ("Moses was faithful in all God's house"—v. 2), says: "God calls Moses faithful in all His house, and thereby ranked him higher than the ministering angels themselves." Thus for Jesus to be the *greatest*, the Jews must recognize His superiority to Moses as well as to angels.

How is Jesus superior? Both Moses and Jesus were faithful. But Moses was faithful as a servant; Jesus was faithful as a Son. Moses ministered in the divine household; Jesus is not only the foundation on which the household (family) of God rests, but He Himself built it! It was Jesus' act in "bringing many sons to glory" (Heb. 2:10) that reconciled man to God and made the family of faith a reality.

It is clear, then, that Moses and Jesus cannot

even be compared! They stand in as different a relationship to God's people as a butler who serves in a palace does to the king who designed, built, and paid for it. Moses can and should be praised as a hero of the faith. But his ministry, however great, simply cannot be compared to what Jesus has done in designing, building, and paying with His own blood for the household of God.

But there is a second reason to introduce Moses here, beyond the great Jewish respect for him. Whenever the Jew thought of Moses, he thought of the Law. The lawgiver, and the Law given through him, were firmly linked in the Hebrew mind. And Law detailed the unique way of life that patterned all Jewish experience. Law marked out the way to experience the benefits of the Old Testament gospel. The person who trusted God according to the Old Testament adopted the life-style of Law.

But now Jesus comes, a greater Person than Moses, with a revelation that moves beyond fragments to wholeness. The implication is clear. Jesus can give us, along with our new identity, a new life-style! Jesus can bring a new way to experience the benefits of the salvation He brings, a way which goes as far beyond the Law as the position of a son is beyond that of a servant.

We have a new identity: sons of God.

Do we also have a new way of life?

Different, Yet the Same
Hebrews 3:7-19

It is important to keep in mind when we read the Old and New Testaments that the relationship between them is that of fragments to the whole. Visualize a picture puzzle, half completed on the table, with many parts spread, unconnected, beside it. That is like the Old Testament. The outline, the basic themes and colors, may be clear. But still the whole is not seen. Come back a time later, when the puzzle is complete, and suddenly it all fits. Things you saw in part are now clear. The real shape and form of that bit of green is different than you imagined; it's far more beautiful and complex than you'd dreamed. Yet, when you see it together, it is clear that even the fragment suggested the whole.

Throughout the Book of Hebrews, the writer is going to refer back to the fragments of truth given in the Old Testament, and reinterpret them in light of the whole. He is going to speak of them as "shadows," which dimly outline the reality and yet are not reality. Through it all, the writer is also going to show us that the reality which has now been fully revealed in Christ truly was there in the Old Testament books, fragmented and shadowy though it may have been.

When we begin to think, then, about the Christian's new "way of life," we are not suggesting that it *contradicts* the Old Testament way of life under Law. Instead, we're saying that shadowy truth about spiritual realities which was contained in the Law has been brought into fresh focus. *Now, at last, the basic, heart issue of the believer's life-style has been isolated and revealed.* From the complicated details of Old Testament regulatory laws, the Book of Hebrews identifies the critical principle. This principle now is to guide us in Christ to a life of rest.

The example drawn (Heb. 3:7-11). Quoting

Psalm 95:7-11, the writer focuses our attention on an *attitude* that characterized the relationship to God of a particular Old Testament generation. These men and women heard God's voice but hardened their hearts and refused to respond. As a result, God was forced to declare, "They shall never enter My rest" (v. 11). In this context, *rest* clearly refers to the land of Canaan, promised to Israel by God, toward which God led His people after releasing them from their slavery in Egypt (see Ex. 3—11).

An application made (Heb. 3:12-15). The writer immediately makes his point. We have been raised to take a position in Christ. Our share in Him makes us the new men we are, and opens up the possibility of a victorious life. But our share in Him will be of no practical value to us if we permit the same attitude to develop in us as was displayed by Israel of old. This attitude, characterized here as sinful and untrusting (v. 12), can harden us and keep us from responding to God's voice when He speaks to us.

The focus in our life with Jesus today is not to be on lists of do's or don'ts, or even on the Bible's revelation of right and wrong behavior. The primary issue, and the focus of our concern as believers, is to be this: is my heart open to God? Am I eager to learn what God wants me to do, and am I willing to do it?

A tragic end (Heb. 3:16-19). The writer now returns to that Old Testament generation, to identify them clearly, and to mark off sharply the tragic results of hardening hearts and lives to the Lord. Who were the rebels? They were actually men and women who had experienced the mighty acts of God by which He freed them from slavery in Egypt! With whom was God angry? These very people who sinned—and whose bodies ultimately fell in the wilderness, never to know the rest of entering the Promised Land. And who does God declare can never experience His rest? Those whose untrusting attitude leads them to disobey, rather than respond to, God's voice. No one who disobeys God can ever enter His rest.

The Rest Remains
Hebrews 4:1-11

This section of Hebrews is complicated by a multiple use of the word "rest" and by a complex argument. We can best follow the thought if we sort out some of the elements, rather than attempt to analyze the passage verse by verse.

The promise stands. This is the thought with which the chapter begins (v. 1). Even though a later, obedient generation did enter the Promised Land, that entry did not completely fulfill the promise of a rest for God's people. In fact, much later, in the time of David, the promise and the warning were repeated: "Today, if you hear His voice . . . " (v. 7). If God's full blessing for His people had been granted when Joshua led Israel into Palestine (v. 8), then the promise of rest would not have been repeated much later to the people of David's day, or by the writer of Hebrews to Christians then and now.

The nature of rest. The word "rest" is used in Hebrews 3 and 4 in three distinct senses. First is the usage we've seen. Entry into the Promised Land, so large a feature of Old Testament history, is a portrait—a tangible example—of the idea of rest.

It was an appropriate picture. God had promised the land to Abraham and his descendants. During the years of Israel's slavery in Egypt, pagan peoples had populated and improved the land. They had built houses, planted vineyards and orchards, and tamed the wilderness. Yet their life-style more and more evidenced the grossest of sins. The time of their judgment by God corresponded with Israel's release from slavery. In coming into Canaan, Israel would be God's instrument of judgment on sin—and would inherit riches for which they had not labored. They would sit under trees they had not planted and drink wine from vines they had not cultivated. They would come into a land where the work had been done . . . and they would rest.

Like Israel of old, you and I in Jesus have been delivered from slavery. Sin's power in our lives has been broken, and we are called by God to enter a "promised land experience" in which we will rest. We are to enjoy the benefits of the work Jesus has done for us. The Christian life is not one of struggle to carve out a bare living in the wilderness. The Christian life is one of appropriating all the benefits of the spiritual abundance Jesus so richly provides.

A second connotation to "rest" is seen in the application of this term to God's own rest upon completion of creation. The Jewish teachers had noted a fascinating feature of the Genesis account. For each of the first six days, the text speaks of "evening and morning." The beginning and the end were clearly marked off. But the seventh day has no such demarkation. The rabbis took this to mean that God's rest has no end. With the creative work completed, God is not *inactive*, but He no longer creates because that work is done.

Strikingly, it is *His rest* (v. 5) that believers are invited to enter! We are to come to the place where we appropriate fully what He has done, and while never becoming inactive, we do stop *laboring*. The load of a Christian life that some experience as a struggle is lifted. The pressure of trying harder is gone.

The third connotation of "rest" is its specific application to the believer's experience. "There remains, then, a Sabbath-rest for the people of God" (v. 9). The Bible tells us that we are to rest from our own work, just as God did from His (v. 10). The life-style of the person who is raised to mastery of life in Christ is not to be the ceaseless struggle some know. There is to be the experience of rest.

Entering rest. In chapter three's analysis of the early generation that failed to experience the promised rest, we saw the critical problem involved their attitude toward God. They heard what God said. But they hardened their hearts and would not respond. Unwilling to trust God, they were unable to obey.

Modern psychology thinks of an "attitude" as a disposition or tendency to respond. Attitudes are always linked to behavior. To say a person has a "critical attitude" implies that in many situations he will tend to criticize (rather than appreciate) another person.

The rebellious attitude exhibited by the men and women Moses led out of slavery also had clear action consequences. When God spoke to them, their tendency was, first of all, to fail to trust Him. And, second, to disobey.

In the Bible these two characteristics, trust and obedience, are always linked. Trust in God (believing that what He says to us is prompted by love and actually does mark out the very best pathway for us) is critical to the kind of obedience God desires. A person who does not trust, but rather fears, might produce an *outward conformity* to the orders of a tyrant. But only trust and love enable us to make a willing, inner commitment to follow the instructions of our heavenly Father. When we trust God, we are freed to obey from the heart.

What then contrasts with the rebellious attitude of the disobedient generation? A *responsive* attitude. When we hear God's voice today, what is important to God and to us is simply that we trust ourselves to Him and obey.

Faith in God, expressed in an obedient response to His voice, is the critical principle which sums up the life-style of God's children. What you and I are to concentrate on in our Christian lives is entering God's rest by making faith's response whenever we hear His voice (v. 11).

The Choice

The talk of "entering God's rest" and the reduction of the Christian life to maintaining an inner attitude of faith-response toward God seems almost shadowy and unreal itself. What does it mean to us in practice?

Pam was recently divorced from her non-Christian husband. Yet she's still dependent on him in many ways. She realizes that giving in to his selfish and thoughtless demands about visitation of the children, setting aside her plans for his, and following his "orders" about the house which the settlement gave her, isn't good for either of them. She longs for the courage to firmly but graciously insist he consider her and the children.

Recently Pam decided to seek a job so she could be financially independent. She's had one or two job offers but can't make up her mind. She talks with Christian friends, and her "decisions" shift and sway with the opinions they express. Pam is unhappy and resentful, restless and yet unsure. She deeply needs to enter into Jesus' rest.

Chuck has been praying about bringing a new man into his business. He's found the person he wants, but they've run into complications with higher-ups in the organization. As a Christian, Chuck has been trying to avoid deceit, but has felt almost forced to manipulate several people to get Barry on the job.

The two have sat and talked and "plotted" for hours. They've thought of this means and that for getting Barry hired. They've talked of what to do if the boss says one thing, or the top supervisor another. Through all the planning and the struggling, each has known increasing uncertainty— and an increasing sense of urgency. Feeling the pressure, neither Chuck nor Barry is happy about the way they're approaching the problem. And neither has any sense of rest.

The Bible says that we are to "make every effort to enter that rest" (4:11). As renewed men and women in Jesus, we are to concentrate on experiencing a "Sabbath-rest" that is designed for the people of God, a Sabbath-rest that is like God's and is marked by resting "from [our] own work, just as God did from His" (4:10). We are to make this our first concern, ahead of solving what we feel are *our* problems, *our* work.

The thought behind this injuction is an exciting one. God rested from His labor because from Creation the complex course of world events has been fixed. *God has already worked through all the problems, found the solutions, and set about to implement them.*

God has also taken *our problems* on His shoulders and found the solutions we need. We are invited to entrust our problems to Him and ready ourselves to act when His voice of direction is heard.

For Pam, *rest* will come when she asks God how *He* wants her to handle her relationship with her ex-husband and her need for a job. For Chuck and Barry, rest will come when they abandon their attempt to manipulate people, make their request known to God, and ready themselves to respond as God leads. Rest will come, that is, *if they maintain a trusting attitude and respond in obedience when God makes His will known.*

As I write this, Chuck and Barry have given their problem to God, determined to abandon manipulation, and obey God whatever comes. And God has already solved their problem! When they concentrated on trusting and obeying God, they were able to cease from their labors and to discover the solution God has prepared since the time of creation itself.

It's hard to grasp, but it's true. Whatever your problem, God has foreseen it from the time of creation, and the solution is already prepared. The only thing that can make you miss that solution is an attitude of unbelief that leads you to substitute your own *own labor* for obedience to

God. If you will trust God and obey His voice, you will experience His rest *and* find the solution He has prepared for you.

The Heart
Hebrews 4:12-13

This chapter closes with famous words that to some seem a threat and a warning. "The Word of God is living and active . . . it judges the thoughts and attitudes of the heart" (v. 12). These are not words of warning but words of comfort.

Law dealt with actions and behavior. Its regulations spoke to what a man did or did not do. The new life-principle (implicit in Law but not clearly revealed until Jesus came to make the fragments whole) focuses on our inner life and being. *God's concern, first of all, is with our hearts.* Are we resting in Him? Is our attitude characterized by trust, and does our trust lead us to respond in obedience?

"Nothing in all creation is hidden from God's sight" (4:13). Certainly our failures are laid bare before His eyes. Certainly the many areas of life in which we need to grow are uncovered to Him. But when we are asked to give account, the attitudes of our heart will be His first concern.

If you are concentrating, right now, on entering His rest—if you are committed to trust Him and obey—then you can both live in the present and face the future with confidence and joy.

EXPLORE

To further explore this portion of Scripture and its meaning for you . . .

1. Read again the description of Bret (p. 29). How would you counsel him from this passage of Scripture?

2. Here are key concepts brought out by the author in this chapter. Give an illustration for each that will demonstrate what each means in practice: never inactive, we do stop *laboring* (p. 36); trust enables an *inner commitment* (p. 37); unbelief leads us to substitute our own *labor* for obedience to God (p. 39).

3. Write two paragraphs, one in which you explain the concept of "rest" and the other in which you apply it to your own experience.

KEY CONCEPTS CHART

HEBREWS	THEME	CONCEPT	KEY VS.	KEY WORDS	MEANING
CH. 1	Jesus' identity	Jesus is God	Heb. 1:1-2	whole, complete	Jesus is enough . . . there is nothing more I need.
2	Our identity	We are Jesus' brothers	Heb. 2:11	mastery, dominion	I need to see myself raised to mastery of life in Jesus.
3 & 4	Life-principle	Experience our position	Heb. 4:10	rest, faith, response	When I trust and obey God I enter His rest.
5	High Priest	Jesus links us with God	Heb. 4:16	weakness, link	When weak, I can come confidently to Jesus for forgiveness and aid.
6	Maturity	Security stimulates growth	Heb. 6:18	insecure, foundation	I can forget myself and launch out in reckless trust that the atonement is complete.

FOUNDATION TRUTHS . . .

7	Priesthood	Relationship is assured	Heb. 7:25	guaranteed relationship	I can have assurance of salvation: Jesus is my guarantee!
8 & 9	Law	Righteousness is necessary	Heb. 8:10	commandment law, inner law	I can trust Jesus to make me progressively more righteous as I trust and obey Him.
9 & 10	Sacrifice	Holiness is ours	Heb. 10:14	guilt, cleansed	I can see myself in Jesus as a holy, not a guilty person.
10	Warning	Maturing takes time	Heb. 10:35-36	process, persevere	I can know that daily commitment to God's will will produce maturity.
11	Faith	Faith enables	Heb. 11:6	enablement, obedience	I can meet any challenge enabled by faith in God.
12	Discipline	Faith becomes commitments	Heb. 12:10	patience, holiness	I can discipline myself to full commitment to faith's life.
13	Love	Faith produces love	Heb. 13:20-21	externals, grace	I can find life's real meaning in others and in Christ.

DEEPER TRUTHS...IDENTITY (rows 7, 8 & 9, 9 & 10)

DEEPER TRUTHS...LIFESTYLE (rows 10, 11, 12, 13)

4

LINKED!

When you talk at length with Pam, you begin to understand her frustration. She knows what she ought to do in relation to her ex-husband. She realizes that for his sake as well as her own she needs to assert her independence and insist on his cooperation and consideration. But somehow she just can't.

In part it's a desire to avoid a scene. In part it's the negative feelings about herself and her own deep-seated sense of inferiority. In part it's her continued financial dependence on him. Together these things seem to overwhelm her. They tear from her that saddest of cries, "I just *can't.*

Most of us feel like that at times. We may be firmly convinced that Jesus is the answer to our wholeness, that He is Lord and God. We may even have begun to grasp the fact that in Jesus we've been lifted out of ourselves, that, sharing in His heredity, the potential to live *now* as God's son or daughter is ours. We may even have grasped the fact that if we respond to God in obedience we'll find His solutions worked out in daily experience. We may grasp all this . . . and yet feel intensely our weakness and cry out with Pam, "I can't!"

Does Hebrews have an answer for this too? Or is the only word from heaven a stern, "Be strong"? A stern "be strong" which only intensifies our feelings of weakness?

Holding On
Hebrews 4:14-16

It would be wrong to gather the impression from Hebrews 3—4 that the faith-response which is the key to the Christian's new life-style is something that depends entirely on our effort. Sometimes we may feel this way. It's almost as if Jesus reached down, held out His hand to us, and then told *us*, "Hang on!" A drowning, exhausted man is *unable* to hang on. He needs someone to hang on to him!

Jesus grips US

His high priestly ministry

Our High Priest

THE FATHER

CHRIST is the link that holds us in living relationship with God

Us, His adopted sons

As our High Priest, Jesus is the link between us and God. As High Priest, He holds us. Our safety does not depend on *our* grip, but on His.   FIGURE 2

In this passage our eyes are directed away from our own weakness, as we are invited to see Jesus as our High Priest. It is because of His priestly ministry that we can hold firm to trust and never need to fear letting go of our new life because of our own weakness.

The High Priest. In the Old Testament the high priest was the man appointed to represent the people before God. He was the man who dealt with sins and weaknesses by offering the necessary sacrifices for sins (5:3). But as a link between God and man, the Old Testament priest was never enough. His role was a shadow picture of the coming Man who would be the perfect intermediary, the perfect link.

Immediately after reminding us that God knows intimately our every thought and motive (4:12-13)—and thus all our weaknesses—the writer says, "Therefore, since we have a great High Priest" (4:14). He wants to warn us against the danger of looking to our own faith-response for the full experience of our salvation. *He wants us to realize that even for this we must depend on Jesus!*

What is it, then, that makes Jesus a "great High Priest" for us?

God and Man. We all know the old saying, a chain is only as strong as its weakest link. For a chain to bear weight, each link must be adequate. The only question that remains, then, is whether that link is "firmly fastened" both to God and to man. We learn from Hebrews 4:14 that the link is firm to God, for Jesus is Himself God. He, the Son of God, has "gone into heaven" to take His stand in the very presence of the Father.

Hebrews 4:15 reveals that the other fastener—

our link to Jesus—is His full humanity. He is able
to "sympathize with our weaknesses" because as
a man He has "been tempted in every way just as
we are—yet without sin."

Some have mistakenly drawn back from this
last idea. They doubt that Jesus can really understand since He was never tempted *to the point of
giving in.* But this is to misunderstand the meaning of "weakness," and the writer's point. *Weakness* here refers not to our tendency to give in to
temptations, but to our ability to feel them! Our
weakness is human frailty: the hungers and
desires and pains to which we are subject and
which push and pull against our wills. Jesus, in
taking on human nature, took on our *weaknesses*
as well! At every point, in every way, He was
tested as we are. In fact, He was tempted *beyond
the point at which we give in!*

Imagine two prisoners of war being pressured
and tortured to make them do a propaganda radio
broadcast. One, after two months, can stand it no
longer and yields. The other resists beyond the
two months, for years, even though the pressures
increase. Both learned something of their weakness as the pressures grew. But only the one who
continued to resist *really* knew how weak he was,
as he daily had to cope with and overcome that
weakness. Only the one who continued to resist
understood the full weight of pain that being a
man involves.

And this is what the Bible says about Jesus. He
knows more about human frailty than we do. He
really understands how terrible it is to be *weak*
. . . and because He understands, He is able to
sympathize with us when we find ourselves
tempted. He understands and cares when our

sense of weakness overwhelms us, as Pam's has overwhelmed her.

The point then is clear. Jesus is an adequate link between God and man, for His personality is anchored both in all that it means to be God, and in all that it means to be man. So we read, "Let us then approach the throne of grace with confidence, so that we may receive mercy and find grace to help us in our time of need" (4:16). *When we are overwhelmed we need never draw back in shame.* Because Jesus is like us, He will understand. Because Jesus is God, He can act for us. Confident of these truths, we hurry to Him! And from Him we receive first of all *mercy* (for our failures), and, second, *help* (for our needs).

If you want to respond to God but feel too weak to obey, don't worry about your need for "more faith." Get your eyes off yourself and on to Jesus. Trust Him as your High Priest to first of all forgive and then to meet your need.

Reach out your hand to Him.

He will grasp you . . . and lift.

The Priestly Ministry
Hebrews 5:1-10

For the Hebrew Christians to whom this letter was written, the ministry and qualifications of a priest were well known. For the modern reader, without any intimate experience of the Old Testament priestly concept and function, they may be strange. Yet they're important, for they speak not only of the shadow pictures of the old economy but also of realities vital to Christian experience today.

This passage begins by making three stateman and its relationship to His present priestly ministry for us.

(1) Jesus in Gethsemane knew the desperate extremity that drove Him to pray "with loud cries and tears" (v. 7). It's striking to note here that Jesus prayed to God as One who could "save Him from death," not "save Him from dying." God took Him from the very grip of death through resurrection. But His suffering extended through the ultimate extremity of dying itself. Surely Jesus *does* understand human weakness! He experienced *all* that it means.

This full and total identification with humanity enables Him to "deal gently" with us when we go astray. The original word, *metriopatheia*, speaks of a balanced involvement. We've all seen mothers so upset at a child's accident that they are unable to comfort or aid him. *Metriopatheia* involves both feeling with the injured, yet ability to react and act for the other's true good. It is neither overinvolvement or underinvolvement. It is a balanced caring.

(2) The writer says that Jesus met the dying experiences of life with "reverent submission." Thus He was able to "learn obedience" from the things He suffered (5:7-8). We never benefit from our trials or sufferings when we react with rebellion or panic. God seeks to strengthen us through every experience of life. Meeting life with reverent submission frees us from being overwhelmed, and helps us grow in our own ability to feel with those who are hurt or needy without becoming so "sympathetic" that we are unable to help.

By learning through what He suffered, Jesus is able to help us in our suffering. Jesus has experienced the benefits of suffering, and knows first-

ments about the priesthood . . . and then going
on to comment on two.

Its function (5:1). The priest represented other
men "in matters related to God" and offered
"gifts and sacrifices for sins."

The priestly and sacrificial system was introduced in the Old Testament immediately after
the Law was given. With the Law came law-
breaking, and guilt. A person who broke the Law
was cut off from God, with his guilt standing
between them as a barrier. For this need, God
planned and provided the sacrifices of the Old
Testament, and priests to offer them. A person
who was cut off from God came to the priest, who,
because of the sacrifices he was qualified to offer,
was able to restore that relationship.

Jesus, of course, offered Himself and by that
one sacrifice holds open the door to permanent
relationship with God. Anyone who desires to
come to God can come through Jesus. Thus Jesus
fulfills everything that the Old Testament priesthood hinted at concerning relationship with
God.

Its qualification (5:1-3). The high priest of the
Old Testament had to be "selected from among
men" and "able to deal gently with those who are
ignorant and going astray, since he himself is
subject to weakness." (As a result, of course, the
Old Testament priest had to offer sacrifices for his
own sins as well as the people's—v. 3.)

Jesus, as we've seen, clearly meets this qualification. He took on our human nature so that He
could be selected "from among men" to represent
us. He was fully human, and thus was "subject to
weakness."

The writer has more to say about Jesus' life as a

hand all that God is able to do in us through our difficulties.

(3) The writer also notes that the experiences of suffering and all that Jesus learned through them "made [Jesus] perfect" (5:9). This phrase troubles some, who realize that, being God, Jesus was already perfect. The solution comes in the meaning of *perfect*. The Greek word, *teleios*, speaks of a perfection that is related to the purpose or function for which a thing or person is designed. Thus the passage says that even though Jesus is the Son (v. 8), to be fitted for the task of High Priest He must also fully experience all that being man means. Having "learned" (in the sense of learning by experiencing Himself) the real meaning and cost of obedience when suffering is involved, Jesus was fully fitted to be the High Priest. Jesus was able, now, to truly feel with human beings and their weaknesses.

(4) Finally the writer states clearly that when Jesus' human experience had fitted Him for the priestly task, He *did* exercise that function. Now He is the source of "eternal salvation for all who obey Him" (v. 9). That "eternal salvation" is our title deed to life now and forever. Having received the gift of God, it becomes our present—and permanent—possession.

It is clear, then, that Jesus is qualified for His priestly ministry. He truly is one of us. He has passed this way before us, and is ready to be our guide.

Its appointment (5:4-6). The Old Testament priesthood was something established by God, and God chose the men who would serve in it. Only those of Aaron's family could function as priests. In these verses the writer points out that

Jesus too was appointed by God to the priestly ministry. The order on which His appointment is based is not that of Aaron, but of Melchizedek (something we'll see more of in a later chapter of Hebrews). Yet the point is clear. It was God's decision that Jesus should be High Priest. It was God's choice that He should become the avenue by which we return to God. It is up to us, then, to come to God by Him.

In presenting Jesus to us as High Priest, the Book of Hebrews has stressed a great reality. We are God's sons now, invited to live a life of consistent faith-response. But we are still men too. We still are subject to weakness and, unlike Jesus, we fail. Should the fact of failure discourage us or lead us to throw over the new faith? Never! The Old Testament pattern realized human weakness as well, and in the sacrificial priestly system made it clear that one who failed was always invited to return to God. Jesus as our High Priest goes beyond the Old Testament provision. He, knowing fully the meaning of human weakness and ever ready to sympathize, is *an open channel to God through whom we can receive both forgiveness and power.* We are to see Jesus as the link that holds us locked to God in an unbreakable, eternal salvation. We are to see Jesus as God reaching down to grasp us and to lift us beyond ourselves. And when we sense our weakness, we are to come with confidence to Him, from Him to receive help (4:16).

Frustration
Hebrews 5:11-14

At this point the writer of Hebrews reveals *his*

humanity. Suddenly he's burdened by a deep sense of frustration. What he has covered in the first chapters is *basic truth*—the first principles of Christian faith. Yet the people to whom he's writing have been so dull, so slow to grasp the great realities on which life in Jesus is based. He feels they have been saved long enough to be teachers of others; yet here he is going over "the elementary truths of God's Word all over again" (v. 12). Infant-like, they need milk. The writer wants to go on to teach about righteous living (v. 13), but the full meaning of the Gospel's outworking in life demands a certain level of maturity.

How do we become mature? Scripture gives us the divine prescription. "The mature" have "by constant use . . . trained themselves to distinguish good from evil" (Heb. 5:14). Maturity comes when we act on the truth of God and thus develop the capacity (which each person potentially has in Christ) to make daily, practical choices of God's will rather than of that which is wrong and evil.

Thus we are faced with a *challenge* and with a *gift*. What is the gift? It is the capacity now to actually live out our sonship, to choose the good that is God's will for us. A man born blind has no *capacity* to see. But we have been snatched from a state of spiritual blindness and given that capacity. As we use it, our ability to distinguish and to choose will grow, and we will become mature.

And the challenge? It is a challenge to *use* truth. Too often, like the Hebrews, we seem content to hear without responding. We pride ourselves in what we *know*. But God is concerned with our "constant use" of His truth. Only when we take basic and elementary truths of the Gospel and live by them will *we* grow to the maturity Christ intends for each of us.

Now, one final speculation. The writer wants to say a great deal about Jesus' priesthood, but finds it hard to explain because of his readers' spiritual dullness. What would he have gone on to develop if these men and women had been mature? Such speculation is, of course, idle. We can never really know. But one thought is fascinating. In other books, God speaks of believers as a "royal priesthood." He says, "As He [Jesus] is, so also are we in this world" (1 John 4:17, NASB). The New Testament truth of priesthood is vital not only because it helps us trust Christ as the unbreakable link between ourselves and God, but also because *it helps us see ourselves as little links between Jesus and the world around us.* As we develop through reverent obedience a maturity that fits us for our task, God will reach out to others through our personalities with His own *metriopatheia,* His own gentle, balanced involvement.

With our lives rooted both in our relationship with Jesus, and in our common humanity with men, we too may become doorways through whom others come to God.

EXPLORE

To further explore this passage of Scripture and its meaning for you . . .

1. Paraphrase Hebrews 5:7-9, explaining in your own words the idea of Jesus "learning" and being "made perfect."

2. Develop from the text and this chapter definitions of the following: weakness, high priest, *metriopatheia,* mature, link.

3. Use a concordance to find all the New Testament references to "priest" and "priesthood" that seem to apply to believers. What do you learn about your ministry for God?

4. Jot down briefly incidents where you might have received or extended a priestly ministry to others.

5. Memorize the first four sets of columns on the *Key Concepts Chart* on page 42.

5

THE FULL EXPERIENCE

It's terrible to feel insecure. I remember my first times in the water. I wanted to swim, but the water seemed so insubstantial. I was sure it couldn't float me. My body stiffened, I flailed in panic, and sure enough, I felt myself begin to sink.

Only later did I learn that a swimmer has to relax and entrust himself to the water. When he does, the water is substantial enough, and swimming is fun.

A feeling of insecurity is always a painful thing for us. And it has a tragic impact on our behavior. Inexperienced mountain climbers have "frozen" on a rocky mountain face, too terrified to move up or down. Unless someone is able to help them, that panic can be their doom.

I knew a college student who, though he was very intelligent, did excellent daily work, and participated well in class, simply could not take an examination. He panicked. His terrible sense of insecurity kept him from using the information he really knew. In every case, insecurity and the sense of panic that accompanies it in times of stress destroy our power to function effectively. We cannot *go on* as long as our responses are blocked by insecurity.

The writer to the Hebrews clearly recognized this principle, and he fastened on it as at least a partial explanation for the spiritual babyhood of the people to whom he wrote. This may explain much of our failure to grow also. We may be cut off by "spiritual panic" from making that faith-response which is the key to our daily life with Jesus, and to our growth.

On to Maturity
Hebrews 6:1a

We noted in the previous chapter that the Hebrew Christians to whom this letter is addressed were hesitating. They had come to God in Jesus but could not seem to break out of spiritual baby-hood. They had not used their potential capacity to discriminate between good and evil; they were not actually experiencing that daily obedience in everything which causes *capacity* to become *ability*.

Now the writer urges, *Go on to maturity!* Count on your new position as God's sons; rely on Jesus as the divine High Priest; and *act* in daily trust and obedience.

Why is the writer so concerned about maturity? What leads him to cry out in despair when he finds them babes, and then in the strongest terms insist that they pay attention now to growth?

Importance of maturity. Throughout the New Testament, maturity in Christ is clearly seen as

God's goal for us. Over and over again growth is encouraged and the dynamics of growth explained. God's concern is not simply that we might be snatched from eternal fires and deposited safely in heaven. God is deeply concerned that here and now believers become like Him.

We saw earlier that we have been given the divine heredity. We are to live appropriately as the children of our Father. "As He [Jesus] is, so also are we [to be] in this world" (1 John 4:17, NASB). God's purpose is that we might represent and reveal Him. Our ability to fulfill this purpose rests on our growing toward maturity. Only "grown up" believers know by experience the meaning of spiritual realities and reflect God's nature and His character to the world.

Two particular aspects of our ministry require maturity. (1) *We are to reflect God's character.* The Bible says that the Holy Spirit in our life produces fruit: love, joy, peace, patience . . . (Gal. 5:22-23). Our personalities are to be developed until in these critical qualities we are like Him. When we are full-grown, we will be able, like Jesus, to forget ourselves and to love others fully. When we are full-grown, we will be able to rejoice in all things, even our own crosses. When we are full-grown, we will be able to rest even when circumstances would create turmoil. Creating Jesus' likeness in us is both the purpose and the promise of the Holy Spirit's presence. In making us members of His family, God has committed Himself to make us like Him. (2) *We are to enter into God's purposes in the world.* This involves us in reflecting and sharing the functions of Christ in the world. Of course, we do *not* enter into His redemptive suffering. Jesus alone died for all, and His death was sufficient. But we are to be involved in the other aspects of ministry. Jesus is the Light of the world, revealing the Father. We are called lights (Phil. 2:15). Jesus is the High Priest, linking believers with God. We are called priests (Rev. 1:6), and in our priesthood we are to link ourselves with lost humanity that men might be introduced through us to Jesus. For every ministry of Jesus (apart from His one, sufficient sacrifice) there is a parallel ministry we are to perform. *When we are mature.*

So it's clear that maturity is important to God. And important to us too. How we yearn to know Jesus' love, joy, peace, patience. How we long to be *useful.*

Perfection? We must pause here to note something important. Participating in Jesus' life and ministries does not depend on our achieving perfection. We need not have fully achieved maturity. God uses us all along the pathway.

The Greek word translated *maturity* in Hebrews 6:1, *teleiotes,* makes this clear. It reflects a school context and refers to someone who is still a learner. With two other words, the "grade" of a young adult in one of the philosophers' schools could be distinguished. The first word meant "those just begun." The second word meant "those making progress." And the third word, the word used by the writer here, meant "those beginning to reach maturity."

This is what God wants for you and me. He doesn't want us to remain perpetual beginners. Or even people who are simply to reach maturity. He wants to see us beginning to reach maturity. And this is what we want for ourselves too.

Often we want it desperately.

If you want maturity but have felt stymied at a stage of perpetual babyhood or adolescence, Hebrews 6 contains exciting truth for you.

A Foundation Is to Build on
Hebrews 6:1b-3

In the Navy one of the guys who went through boot camp with me was named Cantrill. I remember him most because of his total terror of the water.

In boot camp we had to pass a swimming test. Cantrill couldn't swim, and when he got in the pool at the shallowest end he stood there petrified, a look of horror on his face. For him even the instructors made an exception. They got him a couple of tin can "water wings" to use. He'd lower himself fearfully in the water, take a death grip on those floats . . . and sink out of sight. They weren't helping him learn to swim or to float, but he was never going to let them go.

Something like this is pictured in the early verses here. When the writer says, "Let us leave the elementary teachings about Christ" (6:1), he is not suggesting that we abandon any basic Bible truths. What he is suggesting is that we shouldn't use them as water wings. We're not to get into a spiritual panic and clutch the elementary truths of the Gospel as though they were designed to keep us afloat in our Christian lives.

Probably you've seen some Christians who do this. They come to know Christ and are excited about forgiveness. But then in a few days or weeks they suddenly realize that they've sinned. Being saved didn't make them perfect after all! In a panic, they rush back to the altar to be saved all over again.

After a few such experiences, some believers are afraid of risks. Witness? Oh, they might make a mistake. Non-Christian friends? Oh, non-Christians might lead them astray. They don't want to do anything that might lead to failure and to the need to be saved again.

The second verse tells us what's wrong with this approach to Christian life. The "elementary teachings" of the Gospel are not water wings to keep us afloat. They are a *foundation.*

What a difference! A foundation is a solid and secure base on which we can build. A foundation is something that, once laid, we can fully trust ourselves to—and get on with the business of construction.

This is the message of Hebrews 6 to those of us with spiritual insecurity. Don't panic. Panic will keep you from growing to maturity. It will make you afraid to use the spiritual resources you have been given. Instead count on the foundation as giving you full security . . . and go on to maturity.

Foundation truths. What are some of these foundation truths on which we can rely?

•Repentance from dead works. Coming to Christ we realized that our works had nothing to do with salvation and the life Jesus offers. Let's turn away from a "works righteousness" Christian life as well.

•Faith in God. Trusting God is the key to salvation. That transaction of saving faith is complete.

•Instruction about baptisms. In the Early Church, careful instruction preceded baptism. It is likely this refers to the basic doctrines taught and accepted before baptism took place.

•Laying on of hands. This may refer to church discipline (leaders were appointed with the laying on of hands) or to teachings about the Holy Spirit (whose entry into the believer was so symbolized).

•Resurrection of the dead and eternal judgment. These doctrines summarize the believer's hope.

The writer, then, is asking us to believe so fully that when Christ came into our lives *all these things were settled* that we no longer worry about our relationship with God. We *know* that He loves us; we *know* that we are saved.

Warning?
Hebrews 6:4-10

There are no verses in Scripture subject to more debate and argument than those we now come to consider. Over the years four main interpretations have been suggested:

1. They are speaking of Jews who had *professed* Christ but stopped short of true faith.

2. They refer to believers who had fallen into sin and will lose their reward.

3. They refer to believers who have fallen into unbelief and lost their salvation.

4. They give a hypothetical case, used to demonstrate the foolishness of the panic which insists "hold on!" rather than teaching "go on."

To this writer, the fourth interpretation seems best. The writer has insisted we build on the foundation because it is secure. Now he asks these panicky believers to imagine that the foundation is as insecure as they've been treating it. Suppose someone could "fall off" and be lost after coming to Christ. How would he get saved again—what would be involved? We can best see it through this rather loose paraphrase:

"Think how impossible! Imagine a true believer—one who has been enlightened, tasted heaven's gift, shared in the Holy Spirit, experienced the goodness of God's Word and the spiritual resources still to be revealed—imagine him to fall away and be lost again. What will he do to get back to God? Crucify Jesus all over again? Shame!"

See the fantastic truth?

God wants us to know that Jesus' death is enough. There is no more need for sacrifice for sins. By His one sacrifice, Jesus has made "perfect forever those who are being made holy" (Heb. 10:14). *You and I are free to get on with the business of living for Jesus because He has resolved forever the question of our relationship with God.*

The two brief paragraphs that follow reinforce this interpretation. From Hebrews 6:7-8 we learn that the issue is one of fruitfulness. God is (and we are to be) concerned with the products of maturity. Land producing only thorns and thistles (all that *we* are able to produce in an immature state) may be purged by burning. With the old dead works purged, the land may become productive again.

Hebrews 6:9-12 is a word of encouragement. Calling the readers "beloved," the writer looks at the fruit they have begun to produce (their work, the love shown God, loving involvement in the lives of God's people). That they have taken the first steps in the school of faith cannot be doubted. Some are even "those making progress." But progress is not enough. The Christian's hope in this life is *teleiotes*, beginning to reach maturity (6:11). If we concentrate on growing, we too can inherit that promise (6:12).

Oswald Chambers, in *Our Utmost for His Highest*, captures the thrust of this significant passage in a single sentence. "Launch out in reckless trust that the redemption is complete . . . and bother no more about yourself." This is just what the writer of Hebrews is telling us to do. Let's stop struggling to "hold on" to truths God expects us to accept with such a firm assurance that they become the foundation we build our lives on.

Reckless Trust?
Hebrews 6:13-20

Is it really recklessness to have such total confidence in the work of Christ that we forget ourselves and launch out to "enjoy the full experience of salvation"? (Heb. 6:9, PH)

Hardly! Looking back to the Old Testament, we are reminded that God promised blessing to Abraham and to the whole family of faith which should follow (see Rom. 4:16). That promise was itself confirmed with an oath (literally, a covenant) "because God wanted to make the unchanging nature of His purpose very clear to the heirs of what was promised" (6:17). God did this so that we might be "greatly encouraged" in realizing that when God offers us hope in Christ it is "impossible for God to lie" (v. 18).

The foundation of salvation is absolutely sure,

for God has committed Himself to save us. What's more, Jesus, in His return to heaven as resurrected Man, has made it absolutely certain that we will be with Him, for we *are* in Him. Phillips translates the verse this way: "This hope we hold as the utterly reliable anchor for our souls, fixed in the innermost shrine of heaven, where Jesus has already entered on our behalf."

Because of God's promise . . . and because Jesus has already established the beachhead through which we shall enter heaven . . . our salvation is secure.

This is the divine answer to that insecurity and spiritual panic that keep us from launching out to obey Him. What if we fail? What if we fall short? We will fail and fall short. But in Jesus we are forgiven men! In Jesus we are God's sons, *now*. In Jesus we can risk, even knowing that at times we'll fail, for He is our High Priest, ever ready to extend mercy and the grace we must have to help us in our times of need.

When we trust Jesus fully, we really can forget ourselves, and, launching out in reckless trust, go on to maturity.

EXPLORE

To further explore this passage of Scripture and its meaning for you . . .

1. Remember a time when you felt particularly insecure and panicky. How did it affect your behavior?

2. Have you ever felt this way about your relationship to God or something His Word asks you to do? How did you respond?

3. Hebrews 6:4-5 describes a true believer.

What grounds do you find here for confidence that you have come to know Christ as Saviour?

4. Trace the argument of this passage using your Bible only. For each of these paragraphs, state in a single sentence the thrust of the teaching: 5:11—6:3; 6:4-6; 6:7-8; 6:9-12; 6:13-20.

5. Make a list of every indication in this passage that God wants you to feel secure in your relationship with Him.

6. What, from 6:9-12, do you see as the "better things" that accompany salvation as a crop does a planted field? Which of these can you see to some extent in your own life?

6

GUARANTEED!

At this point in the Book of Hebrews we have to pause. We've come to the end of one major section and are ready to launch into another. We've surveyed the foundation truths. Now we're about to plunge into a study of those very "deeper truths" the writer hesitated to consider.

What have we seen so far?

Christianity is Christ, the Son of God, who came with the whole truth to make us whole. In Him we have been lifted to a new identity as Jesus' brothers, sons of God. As sons of God now, we experience our position when we trust God enough to respond to His voice in obedience. Excitingly, even this life of "Sabbath-rest" does not depend on our innate ability. Fully aware of our weaknesses, Jesus lives as our High Priest, to minister both forgiveness for failure and grace to help in time of need. When we come to grasp these truths and realize the full assurance they promise us, our sense of insecurity is overcome and we are free to launch out in reckless trust to obey God, so sure of our security on the foundation Jesus has laid that we bother no more about ourselves.

This revolutionary view of faith's relationship with God invites a much deeper scrutiny. The fragments of truth in the Old Testament need to be drawn together and seen in their relationship to the whole revealed in Jesus. Only by putting the puzzle together and displaying it can these Jewish believers, steeped in the traditions and ways of thinking of the Old Testament, realize how fully Christ has changed their identities and their life-styles. Just *how* and *why* the completed faith in Jesus is better than the preliminary faith of Judaism is something each of them—and we too—needs to understand. Only when we understand the dramatic transformation that Christ brings to "religion" will we be freed to experience the full meaning of our new identity as sons of God.

Glancing ahead, then, we'll discover as we trace with the writer the deeper truths of the Gospel the full meaning of our identity in Jesus. We'll see that identity as we look at the realities behind Old Testament shadows. In chapter 7 of Hebrews, we'll see the true priesthood. In chapter 8, the New Covenant. In chapter 9, the real sacrifice. And in chapter 10, the new confidence each brings.

Then, in the last section of the book, we will look more deeply into the life-style of the believer. Hebrews 11 helps us realize the effectiveness of faith, the key to our experience of rest. Hebrews 12 examines commitment. And Hebrews 13, the way of love.

At the end of our study, building on the foun-

dation laid in Hebrews 1—6, we'll come to finally understand who we really are in Jesus, and how living life His way can make us truly whole.

The New Priesthood

In chapters 4, 5, and 6 of Hebrews, the writer has held Jesus up as a High Priest. Why? Why build on the concept of the priesthood?

By this time it should be clear that the writer of Hebrews thinks of "religion" in terms of relationship with God. Some people think of religion as morality. "He's the most Christian man I know" is something a friend of mine once said, meaning simply, "He behaves in a moral and decent, or even benevolent way."

To others religion is primarily a philosophy of life, a belief system, a way of looking at man and the universe. Looking back into the Old Testament, the writer of the Book of Hebrews goes far beyond these human conceptions. Religion, he implies, is essentially concerned with the relationship between God and man. Its purpose is first of all to open the door of fellowship between them, and *to help man be at home with God.*

The Old Testament demonstrates, as do history and our individual experiences, that man is not at home with God by nature. In fact, sin has erected a barrier between God and man. In the days of Moses, Law was introduced to make this barrier plainly visible.

It's important for us to realize that this was the primary function of Law. Law *never* brought anyone to salvation. It was never intended to. What Law did, first of all, was to provide a standard against which actions might be mea-

sured. It was a mirror; looking at the holy Law God gave, one could see both God's perfect character and man's warped character. Law was not the door that opened up relationship with God. Law was the sign that shouted our need for such a door.

With the Law that brought condemnation, God immediately gave the priesthood and the sacrificial system. The Law was always a pointer that directed men to approach God with sacrifice. The priesthood and the sacrifices offered the avenue to relationship, the door through which the Old Testament believer entered God's presence.

In the Old Testament, then, the term *Law* actually referred to a bundle of concepts and elements. Law, in its broadest and most basic sense, involved the moral code of the commandments, the civil and social regulations that set the Jews apart from other nations, the priesthood, the system of sacrifices, the holy days and worship festivals. This whole system and the interrelationship of its parts was the Law to the Jews. And this whole system constituted Judaism's way of access to God.

Like a house of cards, the Law could not suffer removal of one element without tumbling the whole.

Thus, in presenting Jesus as a new High Priest "after the order of Melchizedek," the writer of Hebrews insists that the *whole Old Testament system* has been tumbled, and that an entirely new door to relationship with God has been opened.

Yet as we've seen earlier, the writer of Hebrews is not saying that the Old Testament system was *false.* He is saying instead that truth was there in

fragments . . . and that when we see the whole in Christ Himself, we can perceive in the fragments shadows which even then represented the real. What the writer is doing, then, is agreeing that *priesthood* and *covenant* and *sacrifice* are important *now* in understanding our identity and relationship with God. But we must reinterpret and go beyond the Old Testament concepts if we are to understand the truth.

What, then, is the essence of the role of the priest? Simply put, *we need a person able to make a sacrifice that perfects us. We need a priest able to guarantee a permanent relationship with God.*

A Better Priesthood
Hebrews 7:1-10

In looking for a priesthood able to guarantee a permanent relationship with God, the writer looks *away* from the Aaronic priesthood of the Old Testament to a better one.

He finds it in Melchizedek, a person mentioned just twice in the Old Testament (Gen. 14:17-20; Ps. 110:4). Here we have another of those fragments that Christ enables us to fit into the whole. Barclay summarizes the qualities of the priesthood of Melchizedek that made it better, drawing from this passage in Hebrews.

(1) It is a priesthood of righteousness. Not only was this man righteous himself, but Jesus, whom he foreshadows, is able to produce righteousness.

(2) It is a priesthood of peace.

(3) It is a royal priesthood. Both Melchizedek and Jesus combine kingly and priestly functions.

(4) It is personal and not inherited. This significant point is drawn from Hebrews 7:3. The

Aaronic priesthood rested entirely on heredity. Character and ability were irrelevant; genealogy was all important. The greatness of Melchizedek as a person is shown in the fact that Abraham paid him tithes, even though Melchizedek did not trace his lineage from Levi (who was not yet born) and thus no tithes were *required*. Abraham responded to his greatness, who he was as a person, rather than legal requirements.

And as for Levi, well, in a sense he paid the tithe too, for he was there seminally in his grandfather Abraham (vv. 9-10).

(5) It is endless. This too is drawn from verse 3. The argument is not, as some believe, that Melchizedek was actually Christ in a pre-incarnation appearance. The writer merely notes that since no birth or death is recorded, so far as Scripture is concerned we see him only as *living*. How appropriate, for Jesus, whom Melchizedek foreshadows, can only be seen as living too.

Clearly, then, the Old Testament did know a priesthood besides the Aaronic, and *that priesthood was better*. To say that Jesus is a priest after the order of Melchizedek is to insist that the old priesthood has been phased out and a new begun.

Why Not Aaron?
Hebrews 7:11-28

The immediate reaction of the readers must have been a challenging question: "What's wrong with the old system? Why did the Aaronic priesthood (and, by implication, the whole system of Law) have to be replaced? Two verses in this passage state the case bluntly.

Perfection could not come through the Law

(7:11-12), and the change in priesthood implies a change in the Law itself. Specifically, "the former regulation is set aside because it was weak and useless (for the law made nothing perfect), and a better hope is introduced, by which we draw near to God" (7:18-19).

Perfect. To understand what the Bible is saying here, we need to recall the idea of "perfect" that we've discussed before. Perfection does not mean moral holiness. Its basic meaning, with "maturity," which comes from the same root, is *suited for its function.*

Old and New Testaments alike invite people into relationship with God. This is the goal of religion, to open the door of fellowship and help us be truly at home with God.

But the Old Testament system simply could not *perfect* us in our relationship with God. It was weak and inadequate because the Law system was ultimately unable to bring us into a relationship with God in which fellowship was guaranteed. We can look at the Old Testament priesthood as having a foot in the door, and by virtue of constantly repeated sacrifices giving a glimmer of hope. But Jesus by one unrepeated sacrifice of Himself threw open the door, and now stands in it Himself, a permanent guarantee that He is able to "save completely" (or "forever") those who come unto God by Him.

The Old Testament system could not fit us for full fellowship with God.

Jesus, our great High Priest, is the guarantee that now we have been perfected for fellowship.

Contrasts. In making this point, the writer draws several contrasts between Jesus' priesthood and the Aaronic priesthood, which he dismisses as "weak and useless" now that wholeness has come. When we realize just how great Jesus' priesthood is, we will realize how completely secure is our relationship with God!

What is it that makes Jesus' priesthood effective where the Aaronic priesthood was ineffective?

(1) Inner versus outward qualification (vv. 15-16). Every regulation governing the old priesthood had to do with the priest's physical body. He must be physically descended from Aaron. Any one of 142 physical blemishes could disqualify him (see Lev. 21:16-23). The ordination ceremony (Lev. 8) dealt only with the physical. Once ordained, the pattern of his washings and the method of sacrifice were detailed—and all dealt with actions in the physical world.

But Jesus' priesthood is not an outward thing. His ability to perfect us rests "on the basis of the power of an indestructible life" (Heb. 7:16). We are safe because of who Jesus *is*.

(2) Guaranteed by oath (vv. 17-22). No guarantee of permanence attached to the Old Testament ministry. But God swore to Jesus, "You are a Priest forever." This oath guarantees a better covenant relationship.

(3) Permanent presence (vv. 23-25). The Old Testament priesthood was held by a series of men who all waxed strong, then waned and died. There was no permanence. But Jesus "always lives to intercede" for us (v. 25). He thus has a permanent priesthood, and thus is "able to save forever" those who come to God by Him.

Once our relationship with God is rooted in this Man Jesus, that relationship is complete and forever. The guarantee of its permanence is the eternal life of the One who maintains it.

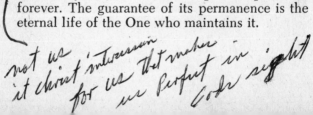

not us it christ' intercession for us that makes us perfect in Gods sight

(4) Personal perfection (vv. 26-28). The Old Testament priests were merely men, who, like those they served, were sinners. Because of sin, they were themselves weak and needed to offer sacrifice for their own sins.

But Jesus "has been made perfect forever" (v. 28). He is "holy, blameless, pure, set apart from sinners, exalted above the heavens" (v. 26). He is no longer subject to weakness and thus there is no possibility that the power of His indestructible life (v. 16) can ever be sapped. He sacrificed once. His work complete, He stands invulnerable in heaven, the personal guarantee of our salvation.

It's important for us to see Jesus this way.

Our High Priest and Perfector.

Powerful.

Oath-established.

Permanent.

Perfect.

He Himself is the unshakeable guarantee that in Him we have actually been perfected for fellowship with God. The task of "religion"—to open the way to God—has been accomplished once and for all.

With that task complete, the whole Old Testament system crumbles and fades away. The shadows now disappear in light as Jesus, the Reality, appears.

A New Confidence

The old chorus says it well:

> We can know that Jesus saves us,
> We can know.
> Be assured each moment, everywhere we go.
> We can know our sins are all forgiven,

Washed away.
That our path is leading
To God's perfect day.

This is the joyous chorus that God invites us to sing with renewed confidence (Heb. 7). Our relationship with God has been perfected by Him.

You and I are at home with God.

EXPLORE

To further explore this passage of Scripture and its meaning for you . . .

1. Have you ever felt uncertain in your relationship with God? Jot down two or three words that describe your feelings then.

2. The author suggests that we are now to be "at home" with God. Jot down two or three words that describe an "at home" feeling.

3. Key verses in Hebrews 7 and 8 speak of the inadequacy of the Old Testament system to make us truly at home with God. Look them over now, and summarize *why* that system was inadequate: Hebrews 7:11, 18; 8:1, 10-11, 13.

4. Read Hebrews 7 carefully and list everything you see there through which you think God wants you to gain confidence about your relationship with Him.

5. Which of these truths (of Explore 4) seems most meaningful to you? Why? Prepare a five-minute talk on that truth.

7

WRITTEN WITHIN

Several times in conferences I've asked people to imagine how they would feel if all laws were suddenly repealed, if the statute books of the nation and states and cities were wiped clean.

The reactions have been predictable. Such words as *terrified, threatened, suspicious, isolated, uncertain,* and *endangered,* came forth, suggesting that human law and law enforcement are a source of stability and security in every society. It's hard to imagine a society without laws. When we do, what we imagine is hardly a pretty picture.

Many of the same feelings arise when the implications of what the writer to the Hebrews is saying are understood. As we saw, he presents the old system as inadequate and obsolete. With a change in the priesthood comes a change in the Law (7:11). Every element in that old system now is revealed by the light of Christ to have been a "copy and shadow" of the heavenly reality (8:5). With the priesthood, the sacrificial system, the festivals and holy days, the civil and the ceremonial regulations, law by commandment has also been repealed.

This idea that law by commandment has been done away crops up throughout the New Testament. Romans 6:14 records Paul's declaration: "For sin shall not be your master, because you are not under Law, but under grace." In Romans 7:5 we read of our sinful passions being "aroused by the Law." Again Paul very boldly says, "The power of sin is the Law" (1 Cor. 15:56).

Somehow the Law, as an external expression of the righteousness of God, never succeeded in making *us* righteous. Like a mother's "don't touch the cookies," it seems only to have made the forbidden more attractive!

It is also clear from Scripture that the Law was a temporary expedient. It served only to the time when Christ should bring in the reality. Then we read, "Now that faith has come, we are no longer under the supervision of the Law" (Gal. 3:25).

Law by Commandment

It's understandable that when anyone begins to teach what the New Testament says about law by commandment people begin to get nervous. The non-Christian reacts, as he does to the idea that salvation is free and apart from works, with the scornful slur, "Then anyone can do anything he wants!" The Christian too often tends to react with fear that, if commandment law is gone, he will *want* to do evil things. Both completely miss the point.

Earlier I suggested that the relationship between Old and New Testaments is like that between fragments and the whole, between part of the puzzle and the completed puzzle. In saying this, I also said that what the Old Testament taught is never shown to be wrong. But it was partial and only a foreshadowing, now replaced by the whole and the real. Thus the critical issue about the Old Testament priestly system hinged on the concept of *access to God*. What the Old Testament priests foreshadowed was the startling fact that in Jesus the doorway to fellowship would be thrown wide open and, with our access *guaranteed*, for the first time we would be truly at home with God.

What is the critical issue, the underlying concept, revealed in law by commandment? Simply this. *God is concerned about righteousness.* The Law is the Old Testament way of dealing with righteous living. *To say, as the Bible does, that commandment law has been repealed, in no way implies that God is less concerned today with righteousness in His children. Instead what it implies is that God has now revealed in Christ the better way to produce righteousness.*

The answer is as simple as it is startling. When is it "safe" to repeal a law? Only when the principle behind the law has been so planted in the personalities of those once under it that they spontaneously and willingly choose to do right.

This "utopian" concept can never function in society. But it can, and is to describe the approach to righteousness adopted by those of us who share the divine life and heredity.

Covenant

Before we can go on to see this concept expressed in Hebrews 8 and 9, we need to review the idea of *covenant.* This word *covenant* looms large in ancient and modern Judaism and in both Testaments. Its basic meaning is that of an agreement made between two parties. When only one person commits himself, it can be translated or represented as an "oath" (see Heb. 6:13-18).

Basic covenants of the Old Testament include the Abrahamic (Gen. 12; 15; 17), the Davidic (2 Sam. 7), and the New (Jeremiah 31). These three covenants are each unconditional; they state what God intends and promises to do. In the Abrahamic covenant, God promises to bless all of the family of faith. Scripture itself calls this a promise and an oath (Heb. 6:15-17). The Davidic covenant adds to the Abrahamic, promising that a Messianic King will rule over the world through a Hebrew kingdom.

The New Covenant of Jeremiah promises to change God's way of dealing with man from that established by the Mosaic covenant, the one and only Old Testament covenant which is conditional. The Mosaic covenant, made between God and Israel, concerned righteousness. God in commandment law showed men what righteous behavior involves. And men committed themselves to do what the Law demands (Ex. 19—24, see especially 24:3). In essence, then, commandment law as a system (1) provided an external standard of righteousness, and (2) required men to obey. It is this way of dealing with righteousness that the writer of Hebrews says is "obsolete and aging" and "will soon disappear" (8:13). It is obsolete because God now has a better way, which we shall explore shortly.

However, it should be noted, first, that the Old Covenant of commandment law did more than teach true standards of righteousness. Under the Mosaic covenant, people were promised blessing for obedience and warned of judgment for disobedience. God made it plain that He can bless men only when sin erects no barriers. It's the same for us today. God's creative reshaping of our personalities, His overruling of circumstances in our behalf occurs when our hearts are in tune with His and when our motives and behavior reflect His righteousness.

This, of course, is the answer to those who fear removing the sense of obligation, of duty, that are integral elements of commandment law. "Then anyone can do what he wants?" No, for God's blessing is not bestowed on those walking in disobedience to Him.

Priesthood Reviewed
Hebrews 8:1-6

In this brief passage the writer reminds us again that our High Priest, Jesus, is serving in the "true tabernacle." Jesus ministers not among the shadow-things of earth, but in the very presence of God, which is the ultimate reality. It clearly follows then, from His superior ministry, that "the covenant of which He is mediator is superior to the old one, and it is founded on better promises" (8:6).

A Faulty Covenant
Hebrews 8:7-13

This passage starts off with a familiar argument which still must have been jolting to its Hebrew Christian readers. "If there had been nothing wrong with that first covenant, no place would have been sought for another." Like the rest of the Old Testament system, the commandment law approach had something "wrong" with it in that it was inadequate.

How do we know that the covenant the writer deals with here really is the commandment law covenant? (Many try to argue that *ceremonial* law was done away with in Jesus, but that the moral or commandment law was not.) But in quoting from Jeremiah 31, the writer to the Hebrews says, "I will put My laws in their minds, and write them in their hearts" (v. 10). Surely the law to be written in men's hearts was not the ceremonial law but the moral law.

The fact that God foretold a new covenant and a new way to deal with righteousness shows that He Himself marks the old way of law as inadequate.

With the people (8:8-9). The faultiness in commandment law is not located in the Law itself but in man. God revealed righteousness, but "they did not remain faithful to My covenant."

This same point is made by Paul in writing Romans. "The law is holy, and the commandment is holy, righteous, and good" (Rom. 7:12), he says. But "I am unspiritual, sold as a slave to sin" (Rom. 7:14). So the commandment law *system* breaks down at its weakest point: the human element. How is this a fault with the Law? It isn't! But it is a fault with the Law *as a system of righteousness.*

Suppose that in your television set only the picture tube is faulty. The TV doesn't work, even though nothing else is wrong with the system. Commandment law as a means of righteousness must be seen as a system too. That system (because of the human element) failed to produce righteousness. So the system is faulty. And God will replace it.

Inner Law (8:10-11). God's change in the system is a simple one. He takes the laws which express righteousness and puts them, not in external commandments, but on inner tables of mind and heart.

Notice that two things are necessary. We must know *what* God's righteous standards are and *how* to translate them into our personal experience. The Law can tell us what the standards are. Only a changed heart can enable us to live by those standards.

To say, then, that a life of righteousness depends on a spontaneous inner desire to do right is *not* to imply there is no need for the written Word. It is through the Bible that we come to understand the will of God. It is through the Bible that we come to grasp the nature of righteousness. And it is through the Bible that we understand the principles which show us how to live righteously.

If you want to experience a righteous life you must explore the Book and learn its principles. God's New Covenant commits Him to help you understand His righteousness as you study the Word of God prayerfully.

Our hearts must be involved in this. We must want to live God's way if our lives are to be marked by righteousness. The answer to this problem echoes through both church history and Scripture. Augustine said it well, "Love God— and do what you please." But Jesus said it first, "If anyone loves Me, He will obey My teaching" (John 14:23).

It is our personal relationship with Jesus and our love for Him that moves us to obey. As our hearts move us, our minds direct us to the way of life Scripture has marked out as righteous and good.

We can summarize, then, what Hebrews here reveals. Mosaic Law does deal with righteousness. The shadow it cast across the Old Testament showed that God, its Giver, is righteous. The shadow shows us something of what righteous behavior is. The shadow shows us that God really cares about seeing righteousness in us. But commandment law was only a shadow; it could not *produce* righteousness. It dealt with externals. It did not touch the inner man.

Then Jesus came. In Jesus' human personality, the full righteousness of commandment law was expressed as living truth. Then Jesus died. And in death/resurrection Jesus snatched us up, and calling us "brothers" brought us into the divine family. In making us sons, God planted deep within us something of Jesus' own personality. "Christ in you," Paul says, "the hope of glory" (Col. 1:27). When Jesus entered our lives He brought with Him *righteousness.* That which had been expressed only in external commands now is expressed in our hearts and minds. That very element of the old system which broke down (the human element) has now been changed.

The outer commandment law of the old has become an inner law of the new.

Perfection. Probably a first reaction to this teaching is disappointment. "It doesn't work either! I find myself still falling short. I find myself unrighteous still."

Scripture answers you, "I will forgive their

wickedness, and will remember their sins no more" (Heb. 8:12).

How is this an answer? It tells us that *ultimate righteousness* is now guaranteed, not *immediate righteousness*. We've looked at the idea of *maturity* often. Let's think of it again. In Hebrews, maturity is something said of "those beginning to reach maturity." It is not the *end* of a process; it is growth within a process. God accepts us as individuals who will never attain perfection here. For our failures to live righteously, He had promised forgiveness. So we need not lose control or fall into despair over our inadequacies.

What God expects is not perfection but progress. Provision for righteousness has been made in Christ. It is this we are to grasp. It is this we are to count on. We're not to struggle to keep an external law. We are to saturate ourselves in the Word, and let our growing love of Jesus move us to faith's obedient response to what we find revealed there. We are to expect God to do His work within, and *progressively* reshape us till we share the holiness of Jesus.

Often a sign-painter first sketches lightly on the blank billboard an outline of the intended art. Then he fills in the outline. When he is finished, the bright colors and sharp, clear letters give their unmistakable message to the world. What a picture of our lives! At our conversion God sketched an outline of righteousness on our minds and hearts. As we go on with Him, He fills the outline in, sharpening our understanding and deepening our love. Ultimately the work will be done. We'll stand before God and the whole angelic and human world. Then the message will be unmistakably clear.

God has produced righteousness in sinful men.

Unlimited Resources
Hebrews 9:1-10

This segment of Hebrews 9 is, of course, related to the rest of that chapter and what follows. But it also has great implications for us regarding the truth about righteousness which we've been studying.

THE TABERNACLE AND ITS FURNITURE

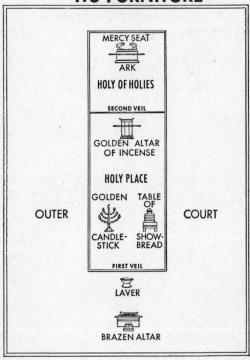

MERCY SEAT

ARK

HOLY OF HOLIES

SECOND VEIL

GOLDEN ALTAR OF INCENSE

HOLY PLACE

GOLDEN CANDLESTICK

TABLE OF SHOWBREAD

OUTER

COURT

FIRST VEIL

LAVER

BRAZEN ALTAR

The first covenant had provision made for worship and also for an earthly sanctuary (9:1). That earthly sanctuary was the place where men could go to meet God. It was a temporary meeting place, and its existence showed that we could not yet actually enter the true presence of God (9:8). Yet every item in that place of worship pictured a spiritual reality that would become ours when the way into God's presence was finally opened. The writer of Hebrews calls it "an illustration for the present time" (9:9).

What realities did the tabernacle furniture foreshadow, realities that help us realize the resources we now have to enable us to live a life of righteousness? Let's look at the seven pieces of furniture in order.

(1) As soon as a person entered the outer court he confronted the *brazen altar.* On that altar sacrifices for sin were offered. Man could only approach God by sacrifice.

Jesus is our altar and sacrifice. When we come into God's presence by Him we have full assurance of our welcome.

(2) The *laver* contained water for the cleansing of those who ministered in the tabernacle. Jesus' blood assures of the continual cleansing we need to maintain fellowship with God (1 John 1:9; Heb. 8:12). Provision has been made for our failures!

(3) Inside the first veil, in the Holy Place, a *seven-branched candlestick* fed by a continuous stream of oil stood on the left. It pictured the Holy Spirit, who continuously lights our way that we might understand God's plan for our lives. We can know the way of righteousness!

(4) In a corresponding position on the right

was a *table* containing food. Here too the picture is clear. Jesus provides complete sustenance. He is the Strengthener, who enables us to live the righteous life.

(5) The golden *altar of incense* stood before a second veil. It pictures acceptable prayer. How exciting to realize that we can come with confidence to the very throne of grace, with both our praise and petitions welcome because of Jesus.

(6) Beyond the second veil was the Holy of Holies. In it was the *ark*, the symbol of the covenant made between God and man. Today Jesus is our Guarantee, He who has entered into the Holy of Holies in heaven for us.

(7) On the ark, resting as a lid, was the *mercy seat*, the place where the blood of atonement was sprinkled yearly. This too spoke of the meeting of God and man, and of access. For us it speaks of our unbreakable link with God, now established in Jesus and sealed in His blood.

Put together, what is the author saying to us? Simply this. Jesus is Himself all the provision we need for righteous living. In Jesus we have access, cleansing, enlightenment, strength, welcome, and guaranteed entrance into the very presence of God when in need of mercy or grace to help.

We no longer look at an external law with guilt and despair, aware that we are unable to keep it. Instead we focus our gaze within, where Jesus lives. Seeing Him, we realize we too are *within the sphere of His enablement.* No veils cut us off from the spiritual resources we need to live Jesus' kind of life. The veils are gone. The doors are thrown open.

Let's enter the very presence of God, and rely

on Him to work His righteousness within us.

EXPLORE

To further explore this passage of Scripture and its meaning for you. . .

1. In view of Hebrews 8 and 9, explain the following verses: Romans 8:3-4; Galatians 2:20-21; 1 Timothy 1:8-11.

2. How do you feel when some rule says "you ought to"? What insight does your reaction give into the nature of law?

3. Answer a person who says, "If you do away with law, you promote sin."

4. What is the most important concept developed in this chapter for you? How will it affect your life?

8

HOLY!

One of my friends has what his wife calls an "overdeveloped guilt gland." It's all too easy for him to feel sick about himself, to relive his supposed failures, and to be nagged by the uneasy conviction that he ought to be doing more. Often he sees these guilt feelings as helpful; he wonders if he'd work as hard if he weren't driven by guilt. But still, the feeling of guiltiness is terribly miserable. And he has no way of knowing how he'd respond to life if, rather than feeling guilty, he felt cleansed.

Many people are nagged by guilt. Sometimes it is guilt for specific actions in the past. Even when such sins have been confessed, the shame often floods back and the taint of guilt remains. Often, however, a nagging sense of guilt can't be located in a single or even in a series of specific acts. People simply feel unclean. Ashamed.

This sense of guilt may move one into frantic action, as if by working harder he can repay the debt he feels he owes. All too often, though, the sense of guiltiness drains one. The pervading atmosphere of shame and failure sets a tone for life and settles down over one's shoulders like a shroud, constant evidence that in fact there is no use making an effort to live. Guilt, the sign and seal of falling short, is stamped on the consciousness and unconsciousness alike.

What can we say about guilt? Do the deeper truths of Hebrews deal with this identity-shaping issue as well?

Cleansed
Hebrews 9:11-22

In the last two chapters we've seen the writer go back into the Old Testament and analyze two fragments of that system which foreshadowed realities that are ours in Christ. Now the Book of Hebrews looks back again and fastens on another fragment. The writer looks at *sacrifice*, and explains that the underlying issue here is one of cleansing.

"In the Law almost all cleansing is made by means of blood," he writes, "as the common saying has it: 'No shedding of blood, no remission of sin'" (9:22, PH). The picture is clear. The Old Testament sacrificial system taught that cleansing was needed by all. The New Testament reveals the true sacrifice which former sacrifices only foreshadowed. In Hebrews we are invited to realize that in Jesus' death we have been *cleansed.*

Blood (9:11-14). Under the Old Covenant, blood sacrifices were always required for sin. But the blood of bulls and goats could only make men ceremonially clean (v. 13). Like commandment law, it could make no change *within.* The blood of Christ however is said to "cleanse our consciences" and this "so that we may serve the living God." Here too Jesus is said to have "obtained eternal redemption" for us. Once for all, He purchased us and brings us out from under the power of sin.

The new covenant (9:15). The new covenant that replaced the Mosaic was sealed by Jesus' shed blood. Christ administers a new covenant "having the power, by virtue of His death, to redeem transgressions committed under the first agreement: to enable those who obey God's call to enjoy the promises of the eternal inheritance" (PH).

Note the impact of key words in this passage. (1) *To redeem* speaks of forgiveness. Guilt is gone. (2) *To enable* suggests that the old patterns can be broken. We can begin to experience now the ultimate righteousness promised as our eternal inheritance. Perhaps you've seen a child's motorized toy, with its steering wheel fixed, going round and round in a circle. It cannot break out of that circular path. Its direction is fixed. We were like this before Jesus cleansed us. Sin and guilt had fixed the pattern of our lives. Then forgiveness came and filled in the rut which guilt had worn in our personalities. With that cleansing also came enablement. Our lives changed direction. We began to move toward the goal of righteousness, and as we moved, experienced some of its joy and freedom now.

Death (9:16-22). Here the writer makes a play on words. *Diatheke* in Greek means both covenant and "will." As in the case of a will, the covenant promises only become ours following the death of the One who makes them. Jesus died, and so all God's promises are now our inheritance.

Perfected
Hebrews 9:23—10:18

Over and over again in these paragraphs a startling theme recurs. We're reminded of the sacrifice of Christ on Calvary. But the stress is on the impact of that sacrifice on us. To see the teaching and get the full weight of what the writer is trying to communicate to us, we need to skim these paragraphs and draw out his repeated emphasis.

9:23-28. The fact is that "now He has appeared once for all at the end of the ages to *do away with sin* by the sacrifice of Himself" (v. 26).

10:1-4. The Law was "incapable of perfecting" those who offered the annual sacrifices. If the worshipers had been *really cleansed*, the Law's sacrifices would have been discontinued for the people would *"no longer have felt guilty for their sins"* (vv. 1-2).

10:5-10. Jesus came in obedience to the will of God and "by that will *we have been made holy*, through the sacrifice of the body of Jesus Christ once for all" (v. 10).

10:11-18. By virtue of His sacrifice, Jesus *"has made perfect forever those who are being made holy"* (v. 14).

Sacrifice is related to cleansing. The fantastic impact of Jesus' sacrifice is that by it *we have been cleansed,* and *we are to see ourselves as holy.*

Guilt and Holiness

It's hard for us to grasp the meaning of this

teaching. To understand its full import, we need to go back and survey what the Old Testament teaches about guilt, forgiveness, sacrifice, and holiness.

Guilt. In our day the meaning of the word "guilt" has shifted in the minds of most people from a biblical to a non-biblical sense. We tend to use it to mean "guilt feelings." "The sense of being guilty or unclean" is most often meant when *guilt* appears in print or conversation. This meaning, guilt feelings, is *never found* in the Bible! There the word *guilt* means actual guilt incurred by acts of sin.

Actually, the word *guilt* appears seldom in Scripture. There are only six occurrences in the New Testament and 16 in the Old. Instead the emphasis is on forgiveness; 60 times the New Testament speaks of forgiveness, and the Old Testament many more.

Forgiveness. Forgiveness in the Bible is never seen as "passing over" guilt. The root meaning of both Old and New Testament words for forgiveness is "send away." God deals with guilt by *sending off* sin, not just passing over it. With forgiveness, the source and cause of "guilt feelings" are removed.

Men have a habit of saying, "I forgive you, and I won't mention it again." The implication is that the sin remains stored away in our memory. We "forgive" but find it very hard to forget. But in speaking of forgiveness the Bible says, "Their sins and their iniquities will I remember no more" (Heb. 10:17, PH). God actually forgets.

How is this possible? It's possible because in His forgiveness God actually does *send off* our sins. Blood-bought forgiveness means remission of sins (10:18). Sins that have been sent off in this way have no more real existence! They simply cannot be remembered against us. Human forgiveness can never deal with the original act; it must deal only with the guilt incurred. God's forgiveness goes beyond dealing with guilt, and erases the very sin that made us guilty!

Sacrifice. Men who lived in Old Testament times lived under Law. This Law, which revealed God's righteousness, also revealed man's sin. When people saw sin for what it was, they became aware of their guilt before God.

The Old Testament sacrifices were a temporary way of dealing with guilt. The Bible never says that these sacrifices "sent off" sin or guilt. Instead the Hebrew word is *kaphar*, to cover. The animal sacrifices of the Old Testament covered sin temporarily until the ultimate sacrifice would be made to send them off.

I read in the newspaper about a woman who lost both kidneys to disease. For eight months she had lived on a dialysis machine. Pumped through the machine, her blood was kept clean of impurities. The machine took the place of kidneys temporarily. The article went on to tell how she had been disappointed three times as donor kidneys were thought available for transplants, then refused. The transplant was her real hope. She only used the machine until the real kidneys became available.

It was like this with the Old Testament saints. The sacrifices, like the dialysis machine, kept them going. But the real hope for life was that someday a *cure* could be found. Someday transplanted life might deal with the sickness from within.

Jesus came to effect the cure. He came to deal with the poison of sin within, not to cover it but to cleanse from it. Jesus, the true sacrifice to which all the animal sacrifices pointed, in one unique act *perfected forever* those of us set apart to God by His death.

An interesting phrase in Hebrews 10 helps us get a better glimpse of what God is trying to communicate to us. "In practice, however, the sacrifices amounted to an annual reminder of sins" (v. 3, PH). Rather than removing the sense of being sinners and guilty before God, the Old Testament sacrifices reminded men of their helpless and guilty state! How? In the same way that every time that kidney patient came to a dialysis machine to take another treatment she was reminded she was *ill*! The machine that saved her life was a constant reminder of how near death was!

But now Jesus has come.
The cure has been effected.

And you and I are to be overwhelmed with a joyous sense of being *well*!

Holiness. It is this sense of being well now that God wants us to grasp as He teaches us that by Jesus' single, unique offering "we have been made holy" (10:10). In Jesus, sin has been dealt with at its root, and we stand before God redeemed and enabled (9:15). The ultimate experience of our holiness of course is still ahead. The Bible says of Jesus, "He will appear a second time, not this time to deal with sin, but to bring to full salvation those who eagerly await Him" (9:28, PH). But even now we are to "enjoy the promises" of the "eternal inheritance" (9:15, PH).

We *are* holy now.

We are to see ourselves as holy.

We are to live as holy men.

Why then don't we? Why are we plagued by a sense of guilt? Why are we pushed and pulled by overdeveloped guilt glands? And, when we do sin, how are we to deal with it? Does "holiness now" mean sinless perfection?

To answer questions like these we need to make a distinction between *differentiated guilt* and *undifferentiated guilt*. And realize God's provision for each.

(1) *Differentiated guilt.* This is specific guilt incurred by a specific act of which we are aware. I tell a lie by shading the truth a little. And the Spirit convicts me. I break out in anger and cut down one of my children instead of building him up with loving discipline. And the Spirit convicts me. I roll over on Sunday morning and skip a class I'd promised to attend. And the Spirit convicts me.

God's way of dealing with this kind of guilt—guilt for acts of sin, guilt brought to my attention by the Spirit's ministry—is quick confession. "If we confess our sins," God promises, "He is faithful and just and will forgive us [send off] our sins and purify us from all unrighteousness" (1 John 1:9). Jesus, working within, applies the full benefit of His one sacrifice, and with the sin gone we can forget its guilt and get on with the business of loving Jesus and living for Him.

Sometimes when we can't quite believe that God *really* has dealt with our sins in Jesus, we avoid this solution. We find it hard to forgive ourselves (especially now that we're believers!), and so we make the tragic error of feeling that He can't forgive us either. Then we fail to take advantage of Jesus' sacrifice. We try in other ways to get rid of the sense of guilt. We read our Bibles. We go out with tracts. We plunge into various committee functions and other activities. We try to make up for our sins and bury them inside our hearts.

What happens then? We learn we can never bury them deep enough. All the good deeds or religious activity in the world cannot so cover sin that its sense of guilt will not spread like an infection through our personalities. How many of us are frantic Christians! How many of us serve God, not for love, but out of a desperate attempt to deal with the guilt eating at our lives!

How useless it all is. And how sad. For God *has dealt with sin.* Jesus' death has cleansed us and made us holy. All we can do and all we need to do is come to Him in faith when the Spirit's warning sounds. Immediate forgiveness will restore us again to a sense of being whole.

(2) *Undifferentiated guilt.* Unlike differentiated guilt, which is awareness of particular acts of sin, undifferentiated guilt is a general feeling of *guiltiness.* It's not feeling guilty about something specific. It is simply feeling guilty.

Usually the general feeling of guilt grows out of years of efforts to bury little sins as they occur. But sometimes the feeling isn't associated with actual guilt or sin at all. Perhaps your mom or dad constantly criticized you. No matter how you tried, you couldn't seem to please them. You never seemed to merit praise. Over the years, the awful feeling that somehow it was your fault—that somehow you fell short of being what you should be—grew. And that feeling of *guiltiness* may very well have come to pervade your personality until your life was blurred by helplessness and shame.

What's happened is that you have developed an identity that colors your every thought and action. And that identity?

Guilty person.

Failure.

Sinner.

Lost.

Listen. *However accurately those terms describe what you may have been, they do not describe who you are. Jesus has given you a new identity. Through His one sacrifice you have been healed. You are to look into the mirror of Scripture and see yourself renewed.* Your new identity?

Holy person.

Enabled.

Cleansed.

Saved.

Renewed
Hebrews 10:19-25

How does discovery of our holiness affect us? We are freed. Freed to draw near God without any pretense at all, letting His blood cleanse our guilty consciences (v. 22). Freed to grow in righteousness toward the hope of complete holiness, knowing that He is faithful (v. 23). Freed to encourage each other in Christ (v. 24).

How exciting it is not to have to criticize and judge each other.

Or ourselves.

EXPLORE

To further explore this passage of Scripture and

its meaning to you . . .

1. Hebrews 10:1-4 shows that the Old Testament system for dealing with guilt was both *inadequate* and *frustrating.* How?

2. Hebrews 10:5-10. What purpose did Jesus come to accomplish? Did He?

3. Hebrews 10:11-18. What was the meaning of the *repeated* Old Testament sacrifices? What is the meaning of Jesus' *one* sacrifice?

4. React: What does this say about my guilt and guilt feelings?

5. Are you most troubled by differentiated or undifferentiated guilt? How does God want you to deal with each?

6. In view of Jesus' sacrifice, (a) how are you to see yourself? (Heb. 10:19-22) (b) how are you to respond to others? (Heb. 10:23-25)

9

"HURRY UP" FAITH

The college kids at the East Coast church had been growing—numerically and spiritually. There was a sense of excitement, a sense of God's presence. New guys and girls were being added to the Lord, and there were evidences of slow but steady change in many lives.

Then came a time of pause, of rest. And with it some began to feel dissatisfaction. They were growing but not fast enough. A nearby church with special weeknight services promised a special spiritual "experience" that was billed as providing instant maturity. Many of the kids began to go, eager for a shortcut to the fullest possible experience of God's best for them.

We can understand their eagerness for growth. We've all felt it . . . and the nagging dissatisfaction with ourselves that comes as we realize how far we have yet to go along the road to Christlikeness. The people to whom the Book of Hebrews was written knew that feeling too. In fact, it was dissatisfaction with their progress in Christian

101

faith that seems to be at the root of their temptation to turn back to Judaism. They had tasted the
good things of God (see Heb. 6:4-6). No wonder
they wanted the full meal! When that full meal
didn't appear after a time, their disappointment
motivated them to look around. What had they
missed? Why weren't they experiencing *full* salvation, *now*? Why did they feel only half way
saved?

Product and Process

It's a natural human trait to want to find shortcuts.
We often want the product but resent the process.

When my wife and I married, we lived for 10
years without adequate household furnishings,
washers and dryers, and so on, as I went through
my schooling and my first years of ministry. Yet
today advertising shouts at young people, "Don't
wait! Borrow." Buy on credit. Enjoy the product
of your labor before you go through the process to
earn it. Just make the "easy payments" as you go.

It's the same with marriage. A young man and a
teenage girl are in a rush to marry. He has no
steady job. She's not done with high school. They
have no place to live. They imagine that getting
married will solve all their problems, that it will
make them different, more responsible and loving
persons than they have been until now.

"I've got to have what I want now" is a tragic
mark of immaturity and of failure to understand
the realities of life.

It's the same in our spiritual experience. Maturity, we saw earlier (Heb. 5:14), comes from
"constant use" of the potential God has planted
within us to distinguish between good and evil

and to live daily God's way. There is no maturity for the Christian apart from steady, daily use of his spiritual capacities over time. The product *requires* the process.

What happens when we try to apply to faith shortcuts such as people often seek for life in the world? What happens if we grasp eagerly at the straw of some new experience, or like the Hebrews cast back to our old way of life for patterns of behavior that seemed to work for us then?

Almost always there is a pattern. First of all the shortcut seems to work! Everything seems new and exciting again. A charged up, emotional high and the feeling that "it" works provides a glow. This is true no matter what shortcut we have fastened on—a fresh baptism of the Spirit, a new relationship in a small "sharing" group, a formula for witnessing, a pet doctrinal emphasis. Whatever.

A little later the glow begins to fade. We can't understand why—we were sure that we had "found the answer." Initially we throw ourselves deeper into the experience that was our shortcut. We join more small groups. We talk even more in tongues. We witness oftener and more fervently. We confront people more belligerently with our pet doctrines.

During this time we become evangelists for our shortcut. We insist that others who are not sharing our experience are missing the real meaning of the Christian life. We begin to feel that only *we* are mature. Only *we* are close to God. By looking down on those who resist our persuasion, we try desperately to convince ourselves that our Christian experience has become fully meaningful, fully satisfying for us.

Finally there comes a time of utter discouragement. Life brings us up short, and something happens to help us face reality. We discover that no matter how much we urge others to find the fulness promised in our experience, the words sound hollow. Inside there's a growing emptiness and pain. Inside there's a cry of unhappiness. Inside there's a question, "Is *this* Christianity? Is *this* all that Jesus means?"

At last we've discovered that the shortcut really didn't work. The product we yearned for, the full experience of our salvation, simply is not ours.

It's important in thinking about this to realize that there may be nothing wrong with the thing we seized on as a shortcut. Small groups can play a significant role in the nurture of believers. Many remain honestly convinced of the personal benefit of prayer in tongues. Certainly witnessing can't be criticized as wrong. And we should be captivated by great doctrinal truths. *The problem comes when such things are seized on as a shortcut to maturity. The problem comes when we abandon a life marked by progress toward the goal of full salvation to grab hold of something that promises an instant experience of what God says comes only with time.* It is against the dangers of such a "hurry up" approach to faith that the warnings of Hebrews are given.

Danger!

There are three extensive warning sections in the Book of Hebrews. They are understood by some to be warnings against loss of our salvation. As we examine them in context, however, we can see that actually they are warnings to Christians against missing out on the full experience of salvation. They are warnings to a people who are almost ready to abandon the only process that can produce maturity.

Hebrews 3—4. The first of these warning passages, found in Hebrews 3 and 4, was discussed in chapter three of this book. Looking back we can see several significant features of the warning that set a pattern repeated in the other warning sections as well.

It's clear that this warning is directed to believers. So are the others.

In the warning, two directions or courses of behavior are examined. Here we believers are told to obey when we hear God's voice. The other possible response is to disobey, to hear what God is saying but to harden our hearts against Him and doubt that His direction is best, to rebel.

Each of these courses of action has an outcome. We're told that if we disobey, we will never experience God's rest. Entry into the Sabbath-rest of God, which has been provided for us in Christ, simply cannot be experienced by those who will not trust and obey. But if our daily life *is* marked by obedience, then we will experience His rest. As the Scripture says, "Today, if you hear His voice, do not harden your hearts" (3:15).

Thus the first danger that can rob us of the full experience of our salvation is presented. We are warned against *unbelief* and *disobedience.* We are reminded that for progress in the life of faith we need to keep a firm trust in Jesus and respond in obedience to whatever He says to us.

This is hardly an exhilarating or startling insight. It doesn't appeal to our eagerness for instant maturity. Instead it sets before us a disciplined pattern of daily life. It describes a process that is to be lifelong, yet a process which both satisfies our hearts with present rest and promises constant progress toward "beginning to reach maturity."

Hebrews 6. This chapter (which we studied in chapter 5 of this book) contains the second great warning. Note that the pattern set in the earlier warning is repeated here, and that the issue is basically the same.

The warning is addressed to believers.

The warning examines two courses that life can take. Here believers are told to go on to maturity. The other possible response is to "become lazy" (v. 12), after a desperate laying over and over again of foundations.

Each of these courses also has an outcome. We're told that if we fail to go on, our lives will be marked by unfruitfulness (vv. 7-8) and that we will fail to possess all that being in Christ promises (v. 12). We're also encouraged. If our approach to life in Christ is one of building on the foundations, we will *fully grasp the hope within.* And how exciting that phrase is. Our hope is not merely for eternity-over-there-someday. Our hope is that Jesus, who is eternity-here-in-us-now, will reshape our personalities into His likeness.

This too is a significant warning for people who were becoming discouraged with their Christian lives. They looked back and wondered if they were "really saved." Over and over again they tried to lay a foundation that Jesus had laid once for all in His death. They were so preoccupied with these foundational matters, which were actually settled already, that they had grown slack about daily obedience and daily growth.

This is common too. One of Satan's attacks on God's children is focused in just this area. You're discouraged about sin cropping up in your life? You're unhappy about your lack of progress in the faith? Satan is sure to suggest, "Well, maybe you're not saved. Maybe you need to run to Jesus again. Maybe you need to keep going back until it 'takes' and your sin problem is settled and perfection comes in a flash."

Don't let Satan deceive you. The sin question is settled. In Jesus' death for you, you stand holy and forgiven in God's sight. But perfection does *not* come in a flash. Perfection and maturity are things you grow toward, with the benefits of Jesus' death being progressively applied as you trust and obey God. Through that process you *grow toward* what will ultimately be the full experience of that costly, blood-won salvation which is yours in Him.

Tough It Through
Hebrews 10:26-39

When we come to the third great warning passage here in Hebrews 10, we find the same themes repeated. God is again warning a people eager to hurry up the process and find instant maturity. God is saying, "When the growing gets rough, My way for you is not to turn back but to tough it through."

The pattern. This warning also follows the pattern set in the others. First, it is addressed to believers: "we" are the subjects (vv. 26 ff.).

Also, two courses are contrasted. The one involves throwing away our confidence in the completeness of Jesus' work (v. 35) and shrinking back (v. 39). The other course of action is, as in earlier days, to stand fast (v. 32) and "to persevere so that when you have done the will of God, you will receive what He has promised" (v. 36). Again a commitment to disciplined doing of the will of God stands contrasted with giving up on Jesus and striking out to find some other way to live.

Results are contrasted too. If people abandon God's pathway (and thus sin against all that the blood of Jesus means for us), they will both deserve and receive chastisement, and lose the benefit of what God promises. On the other hand, if they do persevere in doing the will of God, they will "receive what He has promised" (v. 36).

The critical issue here, then, is clear. If, understanding what Jesus has done, the Hebrews now shrink back and turn away from Him, they can *never* find the fulfillment for which they yearn.

There is only one way to full salvation. The product of maturity *never* comes apart from the process.

The choice (Heb. 10:26-31). To understand these verses, we must remember where they come in this book. They come *after* the writer has explained the full meaning of Jesus' death. They follow his clear presentation of the full access to God, the power for righteousness, and the dynamic holiness that Jesus brings us. In particular these verses follow immediately on his presentation of the fact that Jesus' sacrifice "has made perfect forever those who are being made holy."

At this point in the book the readers *know* that perfection is promised, and that they can draw closer to it daily as they "spur one another on toward love and good deeds" (v. 24). But what happens if they refuse to count on these things as true? What happens if they still turn back—to Judaism or to any of the other routes that are seen as possible shortcuts to maturity? According to Scripture, this would be to "deliberately keep on sinning after we have received the knowledge of the truth" (v. 26). According to this same verse, if we make this choice and turn away, "no sacrifice for sins is left, but only a fearful expectation of judgment."

This terrible portrait immediately conjures up visions of the loss of our salvation. Yet it seems that from chapter 6 on the writer of Hebrews has tried to show us that salvation *can't* be lost. Jesus' death is the perfect sacrifice that makes us holy.

What then is being taught? Simply this. The phrase "no sacrifice (or 'offering') for sins is left" lets us know that God cannot apply the benefits of salvation until we deal with our own sin by confession. It's not that Jesus' blood is inadequate to cleanse from willful sin after conversion. It is simply that even God's perfect provision cannot benefit us *now* if we persist in rejecting God's truth about how to go on to maturity.

And not only this. The temptation to seek shortcuts also opens us up to judgment and punishment. People who rejected the Old Testament Law given by Moses were punished . . . even by death (v. 28). How much more worthy of punishment is a person who looks at Jesus' blood and its meaning and then turns away to look for fulfillment in Judaism—or in tongues, or in "groups," or in witnessing, or in pet doctrines? God says that it is "the blood of the covenant" that sanctifies (v. 29). It is the power of the blood of Jesus that makes us holy, and it is our constant reliance on Jesus, expressed in daily trust and obedience, that applies that blood to our experience and makes us grow.

Trampling the Son of God underfoot (v. 29) by seeing Him as *insufficient* is one of the grossest rejections of God's grace. Believers who do so will taste the judgment and discipline of a God who accepts responsibility to judge His own people as well as men of the world (v. 30).

Exhortation (Heb. 10:32-38). With the warning stated, the writer goes on to clarify the choice involved and to urge the readers to decide for the Lord.

In the early days of their faith in Christ they stood their ground even in the face of suffering (v. 32). Often this meant public ridicule and persecution, at times even confiscation of their property and possessions (vv. 33-34). It was *confidence* that enabled them to live for Jesus then. Confidence that in Him they had something far more lasting than cash. Yet it is just that confidence—that life's meaning *is* found in Jesus—that had begun to waver as the passionate desire for instant maturity had led to disappointed hopes.

So the writer urges, "Do not throw away your confidence" (v. 35). Persevere. Do the will of God. And you *will* receive what He has promised (v. 36).

But *when*?

When will we be what we want to be?

Be what we should be?

When will we know the ultimate fulness of our salvation?

"In just a very little while," the writer concludes. "He who is coming will come and will not be late" (v. 37). *Ultimate perfection* awaits the coming of Jesus. But for now, "My righteous one will live by faith. And if he shrinks back, I will not be pleased with him" (v. 38).

Let's make it our goal to please God. Let's yearn for the ultimate experience of salvation that will be ours when Jesus comes. And until then let's *grow toward it* and live our life in Christ without shortcuts and by faith.

Reassurance (Heb. 10:39). The chapter closes with a word of reassurance. "We are not those who shrink back and are destroyed." The word destroyed is a strong one. It is sometimes used of the eternal loss of the unsaved. But it also speaks of the waste of a jar of ointment, the ruin of a beautiful prospect.

This is what's involved for us. Will our lives as believers be ruined? No! We're not the kind who shrink back. We commit ourselves in faith to Jesus. And, as some translations say, "are saved." Literally the passage says *peripoiesin psyches*: "we preserve, gain, or enrich our souls." The phrase is idiomatic. The word "soul" (*psyche* in Greek, *nephesh* in Hebrew) paraphrases the reflexive relationship, and should not be taken as a separate thought here but as intensifying the already reflexive verb. The choice is *not* between "saving our souls" for eternity or losing them. Instead, the choice is between enriching or ruining ourselves as believers. It's between experiencing now the constant, progressive, often slow but always exciting *progress* toward maturity that Jesus promises, or missing the reality that is ours. It's between involvement in the process of growth, or losing out on realizing our potential because we shrink back from the pathway of faith and obedience God has marked out for us.

But as the writer says, "We are not of those who

shrink back." We've made our commitment.
We're ready to live our lives by faith.

EXPLORE

To further explore this passage of Scripture and
its meaning for you . . .

1. Have you ever felt as though you just
couldn't wait for something? What happened?
How did you respond? What were the results?

2. Working from the biblical text, complete the
chart of the warning passages on page 113. Then
work through this chapter to check your insights.

3. What truth discovered in the study (above) is
most important to *you*? Why? 4. Try to think of
an area of your life in which you are dissatisfied
with your spiritual growth. Based on what you
have learned in this study, how do you feel you
should go about correcting the problem? What
"solutions" do you feel would be inadequate or
wrong to attempt to apply?

question	Heb. 3—4	Heb. 6	Heb. 10:26-39
Who is being warned?			
What are they told to do?			
What are they told *not* to do?			
What consequences follow the wrong response?			
What benefits grow from the right response?			
What is the danger against which *we* are being warned?			

10

BY FAITH

The last thought of Hebrews 10 launches into a new major section of the book. We are not men who cower back and are ruined. No, we are men who fasten on faith and so preserve and enrich ourselves (10:39).

With this thought the writer launches us on an adventurous exploration of how the believer, secure in his new identity, begins to live. With the deeper truths about who we are in Jesus explained, he now moves to explore in-depth truth about our life-styles.

This, then, is a good place to look back . . . and look ahead. In Hebrews 1—6 we saw the foundation truths laid out. Jesus has come with the whole truth, to make us whole. This involves recognition of our new position as sons of God. It also involves living as obedient sons, and through obedience experiencing God's gift of rest. Though we are weak, Jesus our High Priest links us with God and is the source of strength we need to grow.

When we realize how secure we are in Him, we're freed to get on with the task of going on to maturity.

Two startling themes have been introduced in these foundation chapters. The first deals with the fact that we are to learn to see ourselves as new and different persons because of Jesus. This is examined in depth in Hebrews 7—10. These chapters explain that in Jesus we have a guaranteed relationship with God. We have an implanted righteousness to replace the external demand of Law. We have, as cleansed and purified men and women, a dynamic holiness as well. All this is ours in Jesus. He Himself is the source of all that we are and all that we can become. Our experience of life, the very vision we have of life's meaning, hinges on accepting our new identity—and learning to live as the new persons we are in Christ.

It should be obvious that a change of identity involves a change in life-style. Imagine yourself appointed ambassador to some European country. Think of all you'd have to learn: diplomatic protocol, the customs of the land you'll live in, your duties as representative of your country.

Think of yourself merely changing jobs, or elected mayor of your city. There's so much to learn. Your new identity—ambassador, shop foreman, salesperson, mayor—any of these requires developing new skills and behavior. No wonder your new position as a son of God demands a new life-style! A far greater change in your identity was made when you accepted Jesus as Saviour than *any* human change of position can involve. You've gone from being a "mere man" to being one of God's family, a brother of Christ, marked with the divine heredity. And you have to learn a whole new way of life.)

This, of course, is the second startling theme introduced in the foundation chapters of Hebrews. We are shown a glimpse of the sons' way of meeting life . . . the way of faith-response. Now in chapters 11 through 13 of Hebrews, the deeper truths of the believer's life-style will be examined, just as in Hebrews 7—10 the deeper truths of the believer's identity were examined.

The first focus is exactly what we might expect. We are told to fasten on faith, and through faith to preserve and enrich the new selves that we have become in Jesus.

Fasten on Faith
Hebrews 11:1-3, 6

Often when we think of "faith," our thoughts turn to subjective experience. But the validity and nature of Christian faith doesn't rest on either our sincerity or our fervency. Christian faith stands or falls on the *truth* that the Word of God reveals. Thus the writer begins Hebrews 11 by helping us realize that it is confidence in the reality of things we cannot see that lies at the root of faith. It is only "by faith we understand that the universe was formed at God's command, so that what is seen was not made out of what was visible" (v.3).

Much of what the writer has told us about our new selves is invisible too. We can't see Jesus, standing today as the link between us and heaven. We can't see ourselves as God does, holy and cleansed by the one great sacrifice of Christ. But when our minds accept these as fact, and we become certain of them even though we cannot yet see their full reality revealed, *then* we are ready to begin to live by faith.

But faith is more than conviction of the reality of the facts that God has revealed. Faith also exists as response to those facts. The Scripture makes it clear, "Without faith it is impossible to please God, because anyone who comes to Him must believe that He exists and that He rewards those who earnestly seek Him" (v. 6). Faith is focused confidence in a Person who not only exists but who seeks a personal relationship with us. God loves us. He is *not* uninvolved. Instead, He is a rewarder of those who diligently seek Him.

When we are willing to accept as fact what God's Word says, and in response reach out to seek and to experience a relationship with Him, then we have begun to live by faith. And then we will be rewarded.

This living by faith—accepting as fact the truths that we cannot touch or feel or see, then acting on them—seems such a simple prescription for life. Lest we make the mistake of equating simplicity with ineffectiveness, the chapter moves on to detail the accomplishments of faith.

Enabled
Hebrews 11:4-31

In this extended passage the writer invites us to look into the lives of a host of heroes of the faith, and to see how faith expressed itself in their experience. We see as the writer analyzes each life that, essentially, faith *enables*.

Faith enabled Abel (11:4). Aware that God required blood sacrifice (see Gen. 3:21; 4:7), Abel offered a sheep rather than fruit and vegetables. Faith found for Abel the way of acceptance, and "by faith he was commended as a righteous man."

Faith's first enabling step for us is the same. Pleading Jesus' one unique sacrifice, we receive the same testimony of imputed righteousness.

Faith enabled Enoch (11:5-6). The four verses devoted to Enoch in the Old Testament say twice that he "walked with God" (Gen. 5:21-24). One verse affirms that he walked with God 300 years. His relationship was consistent.

For each of us, too, faith promises the possibility of a daily, consistent walk with the Lord, for faith enables us to please Him.

Faith enabled Noah (11:7). Noah lived in a time when all had turned their backs on God. He alone remained faithful. When warned of a coming flood, Noah devoted 120 years to the building of a great boat miles from any sea! Faith enabled Noah to cut through the contrary views of his contemporaries and accept as fact the warning of impending disaster . . . and faith enabled him to withstand social pressures and respond with reverence, obeying the command to build.

Faith can enable us to be different as well. And to build our lives on a revelation of the future that men who do not know God count foolish.

Faith enabled Abraham (11:8-10). The life of faith is a life of risk, of stepping out into the unknown with nothing more solid before us than God's command. Faith enabled Abraham to take an uncertain journey, not knowing where he was going, but only that God had summoned him.

Faith can enable you and me to take risks as well. We can even stand long periods of uncertainty (11:9), for faith assures us that God's summons rests on His eternal purposes. What a solid foundation for our lives! *Faith enabled Sarah* (11:11-12). Here is a most encouraging example. When she first heard the promise, Sara doubted and laughed (Gen. 18:12-15). But first doubts were overcome. Faith swept in to enable her dead womb to gain the vitality needed for child-bearing.

Often we're overcome by first doubts. Parts of our personalities seem deadened and withered. But faith can be restored. Even such "second chance" faith can enable us to experience vitality in areas of our lives we saw as being dead.

Faith enabled all (11:13-16). Sometimes we have a difficult time identifying with great men of faith like Abraham. How good then to know that countless *unnamed* men and women looked ahead, and lived, and died, assured that the promises would yet be theirs. These may remain unknown—but not to God.

It isn't our greatness in the eyes of others or even in our own eyes that's important. Faith enables unknown people as well. Faith enables each of us to count on God's promises—and because of faith "God is not ashamed to be called their God" (v. 16).

Faith enabled Abraham (11:17-19). Faith was of constant importance in Abraham's life, as it is in ours. The first steps of faith led to further steps, until finally the ultimate test came. Abraham was commanded by God to sacrifice his only son on an altar. Faith enabled Abraham to take even this jolting command in stride, and never lose confidence in God. He was even ready to believe that God could raise his son up, even if he were dead, for God had promised that Isaac was the key to his descendants (v. 19).

We too can trust God even this much. When we view Him as totally trustworthy, even the most difficult steps of obedience are made possible.

Faith enabled the patriarchs (11:20-22). Each father mentioned here looked ahead to a future that was unknown . . . but yet was guaranteed by God. Counting God's picture of tomorrow as sure, each ordered the life of his children as if that future were present.

Sometimes it's easier to let God have control of our lives than to guide our families into full commitment to His will. The sacrifice we'd willingly make ourselves we hesitate to impose on our boys and girls, wishing instead for their "happiness." Faith gives us a clearer view. We look across the generations and commit ourselves and our loved ones to the realities He says will be.

Faith enabled Moses (11:23-29). The many ways faith changed the life of Moses are stamped vividly on the pages of the Old Testament. Here we're reminded that at every critical stage in his life, faith shaped him for his ultimate ministry. His parents' faith first saved his life (v. 23). Growing up, faith led him to throw in his lot with the slave people of Israel rather than his adoptive royal family (vv. 24-26). Faith enabled him to defy rather than give in to Pharaoh, remaining obedient to the heavenly King (vv. 26-27). Faith led Moses to command the people to keep the first Passover, and to walk boldly into the Red Sea (vv. 28-29).

Almost every difficult, every challenging experience, every danger, every decision in Moses' life was faced on the basis of faith's obedient response. Faith enabled each obedient act, and the pattern of faithful obedience that emerged made Moses the man he finally became.

It's the same for us. In everything in life we need to be guided and enabled by faith. As we live by faith, we will progressively become the persons God wants us to be.

Faith enabled Rahab (11:30-31). Faith took the godly Moses and made him even more a man of God. But Rahab was a prostitute! Did faith enable her?

Yes, this inhabitant of Jericho, a city marked for destruction, believed God. She acted in faith to save the Jewish scouts, and instead of sharing the fate of the disobedient she became a member of the people of God.

Whatever your past, and whatever your old associations, faith can produce a great transformation. Through faith you can lose your old identity as sinner—and become a child of the living God.

Faith enables you and me. This is, of course, the point the writer of Hebrews has made. As example after example is given, we're shown that *faith works!* Faith *does* enable.

We have no need to cast about for shortcuts. What made the men and women of the Bible what they were was not that special "experience" we seek. It was not the Judaism or Law they followed. It was not the group they joined or the duty they undertook for God. What made them men and women to remember was faith. Their faith, at work in their daily lives, enabled them to meet both crises and drab routine with confidence in God.

It is just this that will make the difference in our

lives as well. Faith will enable us. As we accept as fact the realities the Word reveals, and with confidence in God set out to live by these realities, we too will *become what we are*. We are His sons. We are righteous now, cleansed and holy through His blood. Let's step out to live by faith and become more and more mature.

Good Times
Hebrews 11:32-40

The pathway of faith that Hebrews commends is the answer to our search for meaning and progress in our Christian life. But it's no guarantee of good times.

Here the writer gives examples of victories won by faith's obedience (11:33-34), but he also presents the record of those whose life of faith led to suffering (11:35-38). He tells of those tortured to death, of others mocked and flogged and bound in prison, and still others killed by stoning or murdered by the sword. Some lost everything and fled naked into the desert, to live like animals in caves or holes.

No, taking the path of faith and committing ourselves to obey God no matter what, in no way promises that the circumstances of our life will be pleasant.

I once worked for an organization that held morning chapel hours. One series featured men from the business world who came in to tell us how they could trace their great success to God. Certainly the series was well meant, but it left a peculiar impression. It seemed to suggest that if we only obey God and put Him first, both financial success and social success are sure to follow.

And this isn't necessarily true.

How much I wanted to hear from one *failure* who could share with us, "I have obeyed God. And though my business has failed and my money is gone, I've experienced His strengthening touch. Life is meaningful because I am experiencing even now the transformation that God has promised me as His son."

This is what Hebrews does for us. It speaks to us in our difficult circumstances and in our failures, and it reassures us. Faith doesn't guarantee good times. Faith guarantees our realization of the hope we have for transformation *within*.

And what an advantage you and I have over Old Testament saints. While these tragic heroes of faith won a glowing testimony from God, they didn't receive what had been promised (v. 39). They *will* receive it. Yes, they'll be perfected with us. But for life on earth "God had planned something better for us" (v. 40). The perfection promised them Jesus has given us now. We *have been* perfected (10:14). And in our daily life of faith the promised transformation becomes more and more real.

Through faith, we're enabled to catch from day to day a growing hint of what we will be at Jesus' return when that complete experience of the perfection that even now is ours will be fully known.

EXPLORE

To further explore this passage of Scripture and its meaning for you . . .

1. From Hebrews 11:1-3 and 11:6, write your own definition of faith, or paraphrase the verses.

2. Rethink the examples of faith's enablement

given in the text. What did faith actually produce in each life? What effect did faith have? Write from the Bible text a line or two of description for Abel (v. 4), Enoch (vv. 5-6), Abraham (vv. 8-10, 17-19), Noah (v. 7), Sarah (vv. 11-12), others (vv. 13-16), the patriarchs (vv. 20-22), Moses (vv. 23-29), Rahab (vv. 30-31).

3. Think now about your own life. Can you write a few sentences describing what faith has produced in you? How has faith enabled you?

4. Hebrews 11:13-16 describes the way men of faith seem to look at life. What would this perspective mean if fully adopted for your own life?

5. From Hebrews 11:32-40 we learn what faith does *not* promise to produce. From the text, what do you feel *is* valuable about faith?

6. We all have times when faith seems to falter. Is there anything in this passage that can help you in such a time? What, and how?

11

WITH DISCIPLINE

Counting the cost is something the Bible often encourages us to do.

We need to do so in every phase of life. Chet, at 20, is eager to marry his 17-year-old sweetheart. We referred to them earlier as examples of immaturity. Never mind that they have no place to live. Never mind that they have no money for more than the license. Never mind that Chet has never held a job longer than a few weeks. They must have what they want now. Not only are they immature, but they have failed to count the cost. The idea that marriage will cost in terms of commitment and self-discipline is something these young people haven't faced.

Launching out on a life of faith with God is much like marriage. It costs in commitment. It demands self-discipline and promises a divine discipline that will stretch each one of us beyond our natural human capacity. To live out our new identity as God's sons and Jesus' brothers, we must live by faith. But faith is not *ease*.

The life of faith is a life of discipline and commitment.

It's into this dimension of our new life that Hebrews chapter 12 now plunges us.

Prepared
Hebrews 12:1-4

Strikingly, the first thought in the chapter reassures us. Faith enables us to live a life of commitment. The writer asks us to see ourselves as surrounded by a "great cloud of witnesses" (v. 1). These are not witnesses watching us. Oh no. They are the thousands of men and women of God from ages past and present whose own lives of faith testify to God's faithfulness. Can faith enable you and me for disciplined living? Myriads of men, and Jesus Himself, give evidence: *Yes.*

As a result we're urged to act. Scripture invites us (Heb. 10:39) to fasten on faith and so go on to preserve and enrich ourselves. Then it demonstrates as witness after witness gives the testimony of his life, that faith does enable (Heb. 11). Now we're given a description of the way of life into which faith leads us.

Prepare to run (Heb. 12:1-2). The writer uses the simile of a race. A person preparing for a contest needs to "throw off everything that hinders." There are things in life that are not *wrong* but that aren't helpful. They constitute added weight as we seek to get in stride. The life of faith involves readiness to set aside whatever hinders us.

Let's not make a mistake here and think of this verse as suggesting a retreat to legalism. Instead of thinking of the lists of do's and don'ts that may capture our attention, let's note that the phrase is purposefully indefinite. Why? Because different individuals are hindered by different things. For someone it may be a particular friendship. For someone else a certain kind of literature. For another a passion for playing basketball or for backpacking. All of these are actually "good" things. We shouldn't be too quick to surrender what we enjoy under the mistaken assumption that God is only happy with us if we're miserable. But if even a good thing should hinder our life of faith, then we need to be ready to strip it off and throw it aside.

Sin here is pictured as dogging us, entangling our feet. There's no room for sin to be cherished in the life of the person committed to live by faith. Sin is to be stripped off and left behind.

Once these issues are cared for, we are told to "run with perseverance" the race set before us. Faith does not call for a resigned *patience* (as the King James Version translates it) that sits and waits for fate to overtake it. It demands a perseverance that masters things, a determination to go steadily on. The race pictured here is not a hundred yard dash—quickly started, quickly over. It's a marathon, a run that stretches out ahead for miles and years.

A discouraging picture? It's not meant to be. It is meant to be a realistic picture of what faith's commitment costs. But it's not a discouraging picture. Why? Because of our eyes fixed on Jesus, the source and goal of our faith. If our eyes were fixed on *ourselves*, it would be discouraging. We have no inner resources to enable us to live this kind of life. But *Jesus* is the source of our faith-life. *We depend on Him.* And Jesus is the goal toward whom faith moves us. As we run, we become more and more like Him.

Because of Jesus, our race is one of growing joy.

This doesn't mean the life of faith will be easy. Jesus lived a life of faith Himself, and He suffered. He endured the cross and all that sinful men opposing Him could plot and plan. And He "thought nothing of its shame because of the joy He knew would follow" (v. 2, PH). It's the same for us. Whatever the cost, growing joy is set before us.

And surely whatever we are called on to endure will be far less than He suffered (v. 4).

Discipline
Hebrews 12:5-13

It's possible that this brief description of the rigors of the Christian's life of faith may make some of us hesitate. Quickly the writer reminds us that we really have no choice.

We can discipline ourselves to make faith's commitment. Or we will experience the discipline of God!

Too often the whole nature of discipline is misunderstood. One year a teen stayed with us, a young man who'd experienced little discipline from his parents, and then never in love. Whatever we did to correct or guide him, he couldn't help seeing it as an attack. He couldn't believe that anyone who could ask of him something *unpleasant* could possibly be doing it out of concern.

The biblical picture is far different. Here we see God loving us so much that He is willing to chasten us (and cause discomfort or suffering now) for our strengthening and benefit in the future. God's love is strong enough to act firmly for our ultimate enrichment even if it means temporary suffering. He will move us, even unwillingly, along the pathway to faith's life of increasing holiness (v. 10).

Features of God's discipline (Heb. 12:5-11). The description of discipline given here not only helps us face times of suffering and trouble with courage and hope, but also guides us in disciplining ourselves and our children. Some features of this discipline are:

(1) It is always motivated by love (v. 6). It's easy to think when something goes wrong that God is punishing us. What is actually happening is that God is *loving* us.

(2) Discipline flows out of the family relationship (vv. 6-8). When we're accepted into God's family, He takes on the responsibilities of a father to us. As any good father would, He treats us as sons, providing those experiences we need to grow on.

My youngest son didn't like school at first. But I sent him, and insisted he endure that hardship. School was necessary for his growth, and I would not abandon him.

God won't abandon us either. Even hardships are proof of His concern.

(3) Discipline has a goal (v. 10). Often human discipline reflects adult weaknesses. One parent may discipline in anger. Another will do what he honestly thinks is best but will in fact be wrong. God makes no mistakes. His motive is always "for our good," and His wisdom is such that He always chooses means which lead to the desired result: "that we may share in His holiness."

It's important to get clearly in focus the goal

that God has determined is for our greatest good. We talk much today about "happiness." Often we hear of parents telling their children, "I want you to be happy." God has no such goal in disciplining us. God tells us, "I want you to be *holy*." And with holiness comes a deep and lasting joy that far surpasses anything that "happiness" can give.

(4) Discipline is productive (v. 11). My wife saw a TV show featuring a psychologist who presented a "children's bill of rights." He kept insisting that children should not be made to do anything they didn't want to do at the time. Go to school? Study an adult-planned curriculum? Go to bed at a regular hour? Get up in the morning? East vegetables? No, children should be allowed to do whatever they want, and only what they want.

How unlike God. God faces the responsibility of nurturing and training His children. "No discipline seems pleasant at the time, but painful." Discipline is always painful—for both the giver and receiver. No normal person takes pleasure in the painful. But discipline is not designed to produce pleasure *now*. "Later on, however," verse 11 continues, "it produces a harvest of righteousness and peace for those who have been trained by it."

Discipline or training produces character. And the result, for us, is righteousness . . . and peace.

Response to discipline (Heb. 12:12-13). In every case, the benefits of discipline depend on how it is received.

Our own right attitude under discipline is critical if we're to receive its benefits.

Hebrews 12:12-13 tells us positively how to respond to the hardships or suffering that enter our lives as God's discipline. And throughout the chapter we're given additional exhortations.

The words "don't make light" (v. 5) warn us against flippancy. Let's never try to laugh off troubles, or pretend the things that hurt us do not pain.

"Do not lose heart" (v. 5). Here's another all-too-common reaction. We quit. We say inside, "What's the use of trying?" and retreat into self-pity.

"Endure" (v. 7) shifts our attention to the positive side. Again, endurance here is not a passive and fatalistic resignation, but a steadfast *continuing*. We do not wait; we go on.

"Submit" and "respected" (v. 9) speak of our inner attitude toward the one disciplining us. Too often discipline stimulates anger and rebellion. We feel contempt or hatred for the one who puts us under pressure, and we reject him and his efforts. If we're to profit from the discipline God brings into our lives, we must continually respect and honor Him (never doubting His motives). And we must willingly submit to His choices in our lives (never doubting His wisdom).

What then are we to do to really profit from discipline, and to grow both in holiness and righteousness? "Strengthen your feeble arms and weak knees!" These words paint a graphic word picture (v. 12). Rather than surrendering to despair or fear, we're invited to stand straight and tall and strong and to walk on along faith's pathway. We may be lame. We may even be crippled . . . emotionally, intellectually, spiritually. But as we move on steadfastly in the life of faith, we will be healed (v. 13).

With this thought we return to the earliest

concept in the book, that of *wholeness*. God doesn't want us to live broken, fragmented lives. He calls us to live a life of faith. He calls us to submit ourselves to His discipline . . . to give Him full reign. He does not promise us ease. But He does promise us righteousness and peace. He promises us healing. He promises that we will be made whole.

Are we ready then to call Him not only Saviour but also Lord? Are we ready to run the race that He sets before us? To submit to His discipline? To say, "Yes, Lord, I commit myself to live for You by faith"?

That's what God invites us to do. That's what the Christian's life-style is. There is no other way to maturity.

Ready!
Hebrews 12:14-29

Making the decision to enter the race of faith and submit to the heavenly Father is a critical decision in a Christian's life. Before going on to describe the great impact of that choice, the writer warns against three pitfalls.

The interpersonal (12:14). It's all too easy to let competitiveness and strife mark our relationships with other people. We're to make every effort to live at peace with them . . . and in it all to be holy.

The inner (12:15). Another source of danger for us is that we might lag behind God's grace and become bitter. God's grace enables us to overcome the natural tendencies to self-pity and anger that otherwise would grow into bitterness in our personalities. If we fail to call on His grace to purge us of such feelings, that bitterness *can* grow, and it will defile us. How good to know that God's grace provides an answer to bitterness. Like Him, we can forgive, and forgiving, we can love.

The sensual (12:16-17). Esau, who was such a slave to his physical passions that he traded his birthright to God's Covenant promise for a bowl of bean soup, is held before us here. Surely nothing rooted solely in our physical nature and needs must be allowed to control our lives and thus lead us away from our destiny in Christ.

The old (12:18-21). Now the writer turns to describe two worlds, the material and the spiritual. In Old Testament times, God broke into the material world, and His intervention was marked by fire, darkness, gloom, and storm. Those who heard His voice then were terrified and trembled with fear.

God's intervention was an announcement of judgment and death. Even an animal touching the mountain was to be stoned (v. 20).

The Old Testament spoke much of judgment, of distance, and of fear.

The new (12:22-24). What a contrast there is between this and the relationship we now have in Jesus! By contrast to God breaking into our physical universe, in Jesus we have entered the real world of the heavenlies! We have "come to Mount Zion, to the heavenly Jerusalem." Instead of darkness and gloom, we find thousands of angels meeting in joyful assembly (v. 22). Instead of barriers, there is the welcome reserved for the firstborn son. Instead of being distant from God, we have "come to God" (v. 23). Instead of fire, there is the blood of Jesus that affirms that we are forever linked in guaranteed relationship with God.

We have been invited to stop living as men of the world live, in the realm of judgment and death, and to enter our heavenly inheritance and live now by faith as possessors of heavenly realities.

Why hesitate? Fear of discipline? Good brother, the terror of the Old has been replaced by the full joy of the New!

Refuse? (12:25-29) The invitation to come and live a totally new life by faith is not extended lightly or indifferently. The decision we make is vitally important—to us and to God.

These last verses of the chapter return again to the tone of warning, lest we mistake the seriousness of the choice. Those who refused the warnings of God on Sinai did not escape the results of that choice. Do you think that refusal to accept the heavenly invitation won't mean even greater loss?

And what is the nature of that loss? Loss of salvation? Of course not. Instead God turns our attention to permanence. He has made a promise. God will shake both heavens and earth with a mighty shaking that marks the destruction of the physical universe and everything in it. Only the uncreated, which cannot be shaken, will remain.

The implications are clear. *Will you and I choose to turn away from faith's life, and build our hopes on the success, the power, the wealth, the pleasures, offered us in the created universe? If so, beware. For all these things will be dissolved. And then when God shakes the universe out of its tenuous existence, we will have nothing left!*

Let's hear His voice today. Let's not refuse. Let's build our lives on things that cannot be shaken and that will always remain.

And so the closing words. When we live our new identity by faith, "we are receiving a kingdom that cannot be shaken" (v. 28). So let's be thankful. Let's worship God with reverence and awe. And let's remember who our God is.

A consuming fire.

EXPLORE

To further explore this passage of Scripture and its meaning to you . . .

1. Think how some person you know has given you witness of the enabling of faith. How has he or she encouraged you to trust?

2. Study Hebrews 12:5-13 carefully, and record:

    a. What do I learn here about God?

    b. What do I learn here about my role as His child?

    c. What do I learn here about my role as a parent?

    d. What do I learn here about my own children?

3. Which of the "learnings" from 2 (above) is most important to you now? Why?

4. Looking at Hebrews 12:14-17, try to think of a personal example of how each problem area exposed can hinder you spiritually.

5. Think about the motivations to encourage commitment to the faith-life in 12:18-29. Which of them do you feel would be most likely to motivate you? Why?

12

IN LOVE

One of the most visible and meaningful marks of the life of faith is love. It's exciting for us that this is so. We all yearn for love. And we need love—both to give it and receive it. Probably few passages in Scripture are as familiar today as that in which Jesus laid down His new commandment, "Love one another" (John 13:34).

Launching out into the life of faith will most certainly mean a new experience of love for you. A new warmth in your relationships with other people. A new capacity to care for other people, and a new awareness of their warm support.

What a wonderful theme with which to close the Book of Hebrews. These people had been ready to turn back. They were missing something. Their lives were seemingly growing empty. In response the writer has turned their attention to the towering truths of who they are in Jesus. Their new identity established, he challenged them with a blunt description of the path on which commitment and discipline would lead

136

them. And now, in closing, he speaks of love. He explores the *relationships*, with others and with God, that transform one's experience and provide joy.

For this, you see, is what remains when all else is shaken. The whole material universe will flare up and after a moment of intense heat disappear, leaving not even dust (2 Peter 3:10). And what will remain?

You.

And me.

Other people.

And God.

To invest our lives in that which cannot be shaken means to invest our lives in one another. When all else has gone, the impact which love has had in shaping others toward God will forever remain.

Love's Way
Hebrews 13:1-8

The chapter begins with a brief survey of some of the relationships we can now experience as faith enables us.

Brothers (13:1). "Keep on loving each other as brothers." Our new relationship with Jesus as our brother gives us a new relationship with all of God's children. We're in the family together. Never alone again, we have many brothers and sisters with whom to share. This relationship is something we're never to forget.

It's easy to think of the man in the pew across the aisle as "that Calvinist." Or "that dispensationalist." Or "that legalist." Or even as "that unfriendly fellow." But all such classifications

fade to insignificance before the one basic identity we share. "That *brother*."

Recognizing who *we* are, and who others are,
we are to "keep on loving each other, *as brothers*."

Strangers (13:2). Our love isn't limited to the
family. We're to love even strangers. Jesus makes
it even stronger. "Love your enemies" (Matt.
5:44).

The writer adds an interesting reminder here.
"For by doing so some people have entertained
angels without knowing it." The application is
simple. When you meet a stranger, you cannot tell
who he may turn out to be. We meet people daily
who are strangers to God and strangers to God's
family. But we cannot tell who they will turn out
to be. Through our welcome they may well
become brothers.

Sufferers (13:3). Love is never impersonal or
unconcerned. Real love is always involved,
though not so involved that perspective is lost
and we cannot do what is best for others. But
involved enough to *feel with* others who are
mistreated and in need.

Perhaps this verse refers to fellow-believers
who were undergoing official persecution. But the
principle is broader. If we are to really care, we
need to empathize. We need to be involved.

This kind of relationship is costly, but it brings
rich rewards.

Mate (13:4). Most love relationships in the
family of God are inclusive. There's love enough
in Jesus for us to care about all our brothers and
sisters. But there are exclusive relationships as
well. And there are valid and invalid ways to
express love.

Church history shows that people have at times

gone beyond the valid expressions of love to encourage sexual involvements to "enrich" the fellowship of so-called believers. The writer of Hebrews has two comments to make.

First, honor marriage. Don't ever feel that human sexuality is *un*spiritual or that this closest of human relationships cannot be a part of the believer's discovery of the meaning of God's love.

Second, realize that the values of sex are *limited* to marriage. Sexual immorality is something that God will most certainly judge.

Things (13:5a). "Love" is often distorted in human lives, distorted by being focused on the wrong objects. Just as we are to focus on other persons because it is people who will remain when all else has been shaken, we are warned against developing desires for empty things. "Keep your lives free from the love of money" warns us to remember that people, not cash, are to be important to us. Only in developing those relationships with God and others that provide lasting meaning for human life can our destiny be found.

With material things in perspective, we're directed elsewhere to locate our security and our contentment. We're told, "Be content with what you have," and then told the liberating reason this is possible:

"Never will I leave you;
Never will I forsake you."

Our relationship with God is a forever thing, and knowing Him is the basis for our sense of security.

A friend tells of an acquaintance who finds it difficult to feel secure. Though wealthy, this widow is unable to relax unless she has at least

$20,000 in her possession, in cash, at all times. How tragic a dependence. At best, wealth is fleeting. At worst, it is deceiving. How good it is that we can depend on God, who has made a permanent commitment to be with us and who is able to meet our every need.

Opponents (13:6). The relationship we have with the Lord is as vital a source of confidence and security as the relationships we will develop with others in God's family. Because the Lord is our helper, we never need to fear man.

Leaders (13:7). God has given His church leaders to set the spiritual pace. This verse focuses our attention on love's way with them. We are to remember them, and, considering "the outcome of their way of life," we are to "imitate their faith."

It's interesting to note that we are not asked to imitate their accomplishments. Or their activities. What we're to imitate is their *faith*. God leads each of us down different roads to find our own place in life. We're wrong if we "try to be like Billy Graham and become an evangelist." What is significant is not what a particular leader *does*, but the evidence from his life that faith's way is profitable. Leaders become who they are through faith.

Jesus (13:8). Undergirding every relationship is our relationship with Jesus, who is "the same yesterday and today and forever." Whatever changes life may bring in our relationships, through moving our residence, through death, through desertion, nothing can make obsolete our relationship with Jesus, for He remains the same.

His love is constant.

His love is ours.

Outside the camp
Hebrews 13:9-16

In this concluding chapter, the writer returns to an earlier thought. The shadows are gone. Our lives are no longer to be built on form and habit, on externals and empty behavior. "Do not be carried away by all kinds of strange teaching," he writes. "Our hearts are to be strengthened by grace, not by ceremonial foods."

We have such a tendency to look to externals as marks of spirituality or as aids to spiritual growth. If I just do this. Or go there. Or spend more time on that. *But looking to things outside us is futile! We are to look to Jesus, who links us to God from within. And when we hear His voice, we are to respond with faith and obedience. This and this alone is the issue out of which our Christian life finds its shape and its maturity.* This inner altar is one at which those who persist in chasing shadows have no right and no share (v. 10).

Now comes a final, compelling picture. In the Old Testament economy, the high priest offered the sacrificial blood in the Most Holy Place. But the carcasses were burned outside the city. This the writer tells us is a picture of Jesus who also "suffered outside the city gate" (v. 12). And, the writer urges, let us "go to Him outside the camp" (v. 13).

Let us turn our backs on all the now empty forms and means of grace that reflect the old shadow system. Let us go *outside* that whole system, outside the city which was its center, and let us go to Jesus. Let's find *in Him* the reality that everything else only pictures. And, having the reality, let's realize that we have no more need of shadows.

"Through Jesus, therefore," the thought concludes, "let us continually offer to God a sacrifice of praise" (v. 15). Through Jesus, let's do good and share with others (v. 16). Through Jesus, and through Jesus *alone*, let's go on to discover the full meaning of being saved.

Farewell
Hebrews 13:17-22

A few scattered thoughts mark the close of this towering epistle.

Obey your leaders (13:17). Make their ministry a joy by responding to them warmly, as you respond to God, who has given them their ministry.

Pray for us (13:18). Even a man who writes on maturity remains in need of support and prayer. He needs to maintain a clear conscience and a passion to live honorably in every way. And he needs the presence and fellowship of others: "I particularly urge you to pray so that I may be restored to you soon."

With thoughts of Timothy, with greetings, with encouragement to heed the short letter he had penned, the writer adds a benediction that stands as one of the greatest masterpieces of Scripture. And it is one of the great promises for us.

Because of Jesus, and through faith, this benediction can become reality in our lives: "May the God of peace, who through the blood of the eternal covenant brought back from the dead our Lord Jesus, that great Shepherd of the sheep, equip you with everything good for doing His will, and may He work in us what is pleasing to Him, through Jesus Christ, to whom be glory forever and ever. Amen."

That benediction tells you who you have become.

And what it means not to be just halfway but all the way saved.

EXPLORE

To further explore this passage and its meaning for you . . .

1. On a piece of paper, draw a circle that represents you. Then, around it, at various distances, draw other circles to represent other people, letting the size of the circles show their importance to you, and the distance show how secure you feel in your relationship with them.

What does this piece of paper tell you about love and you?

2. Look over Hebrews 13:1-8. How can any of its injunctions be applied to the relationships you diagramed for 1 (above)? How do principles in the text explain positive relationships you now have? How do principles in the text explain poor relationships, or guide you in changing them?

3. What are some of the "external" things you may have been depending on as keys to your relationship with God? (Heb. 13:9-16) What would going outside the camp (abandoning the shadows) mean for you? Would it be easy or hard?

4. From your understanding of Hebrews, what do you believe God intends to replace the external props many of us lean on?

5. Examine the benediction of 13:20-21. What themes from Hebrews do you see reflected here? What portrait of maturity and "full salvation"

does it give? What seem to be the resources recommended as able to produce this dramatic transformation?

6. Finally, how has your own life changed as you've studied this book? Have you heard God's voice in any significant way? How have you responded? If you've missed hearing His voice, or failed to respond, study Hebrews again! For through it God wants to speak . . . to you!